Railway Co. Cape Fear a. Yadkin Valley

Charter of the Cape Fear and Yadkin Valley Railway Co.

formerly Western Railroad Company : and acts amendatory thereto to

March 26, 1880 : also charter and amendatory acts relating to the Mount

Airy Rail Road Company

Railway Co. Cape Fear a. Yadkin Valley

Charter of the Cape Fear and Yadkin Valley Railway Co.
formerly Western Railroad Company : and acts amendatory thereto to March 26,
1880 : also charter and amendatory acts relating to the Mount Airy Rail Road
Company

ISBN/EAN: 9783337735012

Printed in Europe, USA, Canada, Australia, Japan

Cover: Foto ©Andreas Hilbeck / pixelio.de

More available books at **www.hansebooks.com**

CHARTER

OF THE

CAPE FEAR

AND

Yadkin Valley Railway Co.,

FORMERLY

WESTERN RAILROAD COMPANY,

AND ACTS AMENDATORY THERETO TO MARCH 26, 1880.

—ALSO—

CHARTER AND AMENDATORY ACTS RELATING TO THE
MOUNT AIRY RAIL ROAD COMPANY, (NOW CON-
SOLIDATED WITH THE CAPE FEAR AND
YADKIN VALLEY RAILWAY CO.)

TOGETHER WITH THE

BY-LAWS AND AN APPENDIX,

CONTAINING LAWS RELATING TO RAILROADS, APPLICABLE TO
THE CAPE FEAR AND YADKIN VALLEY RAILWAY CO.

RALEIGH:
EDWARDS, BROUGHTON & CO., PRINTERS AND BINDERS.
1881.

CHARTER

OF THE

Western Railroad Company.

An Act to incorporate a company to construct a Railroad from some point on the Cape Fear river at or near Fayetteville, to some point in the Coal Regions, hereafter to be determined.

SECTION 1. *Be it enacted by the General Assembly of the State of North Carolina, and it is hereby enacted by the authority of the same,* That for the purpose of establishing a communication by Railroad, between the town of Fayetteville and the coal region in the counties of Moore and Chatham, at some point to be hereafter determined, the formation of a corporate Company, with a capital of five hundred thousand dollars, is hereby authorized, to be called "The Western Railroad Company," and when formed, in compliance with the conditions hereinafter prescribed, to have a corporate existence as a body politic in perpetuity.

SEC. 2. *Be it further enacted,* The said Company be, and the same is hereby authorized to construct a Railroad from the town of Fayetteville to some point in the coal region, in the county of Moore, or in the county of Chatham, to be determined by said Company after the same shall have been formed.

SEC. 3. *Be it further enacted,* That for the purpose of raising the capital stock of said Company, it shall be lawful to open books in the town of Fayetteville, under the direction of the following Commissioners, to-wit: Duncan G. McRae, Jesse G. Shepherd, James Kyle, William H. Haigh, John Eccles, Geo. McNeill, Thos. S. Lutterloh, John H. Cook, Edward J. Hale, Benj. W. Robinson, Robt. K. Bryan, Robert Strange and David A. Ray; in the town of Wilmington, under the direction of P. K. Dickinson, Thos. H. Wright, Jno. A. Taylor, Gilbert Potter, Jno. McRae, Sen., O. G. Pars-

ley, A. J. DeRossett, Jun., Robert W. Brown and D. K. Mc-
Rae, and at such other places, and under the direction of
such persons as a majority of the Commissioners first above
named may deem proper, for the purpose of receiving subscriptions to an amount not exceeding five hundred thousand dollars, in shares of one hundred dollars each.

SEC. 4. *Be it further enacted*, That the Commissioners
above named, and all other persons who may hereafter be
authorized as aforesaid to open books for subscriptions, shall
open .the same at any time after the ratification of this act,
first giving twenty days' notice thereof of the time and place
in one or more of the newspapers printed in Fayetteville
and Wilmington, and the said books, when open, shall be
kept open for the space of sixty days at least, and as long
thereafter as the Commissioners first above named shall direct; and the said first named Commissioners shall have
power to call on and require all persons empowered to receive subscriptions of stock, at any time and from time to
time, as a majority of them may think proper, to make return of the subscriptions of stock by them respectively received.

SEC. 5. *Be it further enacted*, That whenever the .sum of
one hundred thousand dollars shall be subscribed in manner and form aforesaid, the subscribers, their executors, administrators or assigns, shall be and they are hereby declared incorporated into a Company by the name and style
of the "Western Railroad Company," and by that name
shall be capable in law and equity of purchasing, holding,
selling, leasing and conveying estates, real, personal and
mixed, and of acquiring the same by gift or devise, so far as
shall be necessary for the purposes embraced within the
scope, object and interest [intent] of their charter and no
further, and shall have perpetual succession; and by their
corporate name may sue and be sued, plead and be im-
pleaded in any court of law and equity in this State, and
may have and use a common seal, which they may alter
and renew at pleasure, and shall have and enjoy all other
rights and immunities which other corporate bodies may
and of right do exercise, and make all such by-laws, rules
and regulations as are necessary for the government of the
corporation, or effecting the object for which it was created,
not inconsistent with the Constitution and laws of the State.

SEC. 6. *Be it further enacted*, That it shall be the duty of
the Commissioners named in this act for receiving subscriptions in Fayetteville, or a majority of them, as soon as the

sum of one hundred thousand dollars shall have been subscribed in manner aforesaid, to give public notice thereof,
and at the same time call a general meeting of the stockholders, giving at least thirty days' notice of the time and
place of meeting, at which meeting a majority of the stockholders being represented in person or by proxy, shall proceed to elect a President and Treasurer, and nine Directors
out of the number of stockholders; and the said Directors
shall have power to perform all the duties necessary for the
government of the corporation and the transaction of its
business; and the persons elected as aforesaid shall serve such
period, not exceeding one year, as the stockholders may direct; and at that meeting the stockholders shall fix on the
day and place or places where the subsequent election of
President, Treasurer and Directors shall be held, and such
elections shall thenceforth be annually made; but if the
day of the annual election of officers should, under any cir-
cumstances, pass without an election, the corporation shall
not thereby be dissolved, but the officers formerly elected
shall continue in office until a new election takes place.

SEC. 7. *Be it further enacted,* That the selection of officers
aforesaid shall be by ballot, each stockholder having as
many votes as he has shares in the stock of the Company,
and the person having the greatest number of votes polled
shall be considered duly elected to the office for which he is
nominated, and at all elections, and upon all votes taken at
any meeting of the stockholders upon any by-law or any of
the affairs of the Company, each share of stock shall be entitled to one vote, to be represented either in person or by
proxy, and proxies may be verified in such manner as the
by-laws of the Company prescribe.

SEC. 8. *Be it further enacted,* That the Board of Directors
may fill any vacancies which may occur in it during the
period for which they have been elected, and in the absence
of the President may appoint a President *pro tempore* to fill
his place.

SEC. 9. *Be it further enacted,* That the Board of Directors
may call for the sums subscribed as stock in said Company
in such installments as the interest of said Company may,
in their opinion, require; the call for each payment shall be
published in one or more newspapers of the State for one
month before the day of payment, and on failure of any
stockholder to pay each installments as thus required, the
Directors may sell at public auction, on a previous notice of
ten days, for cash, all the stock subscribed for in said Com-

pany by such stockholder, and convey the same to the purchaser at said sale, and if the said sale of stock do not produce a sum sufficient to pay off the incidental expenses of the sale, and the entire amount owing by such stockholder to the Company for such subscription of stock, then and in that case, the whole of such balance shall be held as due at once to the Company, and may be recovered of such stockholder or his executor, administrator or assigns at the suit of said Company, either by summary motion in any court of superior jurisdiction in the County where the delinquent resides, on previous notice of ten days to said subscriber, or by the action of *assumpsit* in any court of competent jurisdiction, or by warrant before a Justice of the Peace, where the sum does not exceed one hundred dollars, and in all cases of assignment of stock, before the whole amount is paid to the Company, then for all sums due on such stock, both the original subscriber and the first and all subsequent assignees shall be liable to the Company, and the same may be recovered as above described.

Sec. 10. *Be it further enacted*, That the debt of the stockholders due to the Company for stock therein, either as original proprietor or as a first or subsequent assignee, shall be considered as of equal dignity with judgments in the distribution of assets of a deceased stockholder by his legal representatives.

Sec. 11. *Be it further enacted*, That the said Company shall issue certificates of stock to its members, and said stock may be transferred in such manner and form as may be directed by the by-laws of the Company.

Sec. 12. *Be it further enacted*, That the said Company may, at any time, increase its capital stock to a sum sufficient to complete said Road, not exceeding the additional sum of five hundred thousand dollars, by opening books for the subscription of new stock or borrowing money on the credit of the Company and on the mortgage of its charter and works, and the manner in which the same shall be done in either case shall be prescribed by the stockholders.

Sec. 13. *Be it further enacted*, That the said Company shall have power of using any section of the said Road constructed by them before the whole of said Road shall be completed, and may charge for transportation thereon.

Sec. 14. *Be it further enacted*, That all contracts or agreements authenticated by the President and Secretary of the Board shall be binding on the Company, with or without a seal. Such a mode of authentication shall be used as the Company by their by-laws may adopt.

SEC. 15. *Be it further enacted*, That the said Company may purchase, have and hold in fee or for a term of years any lands, tenements or hereditaments which may be necessary for the said Road, or for the erection of depositories, store-houses, houses for the officers, servants or agents of the Company, or for workshops or foundries to be used by the Company, or for procuring stone or other material necessary to the construction of the Road, or effecting transportation, and for no other purpose whatever.

SEC. 16. *Be it further enacted*, That the Company shall have the right, when necessary, to construct the said Rail Road across any public road or along the side of any public road : *Provided*, That the said Company shall not obstruct any public road without first constructing one equally as good and as convenient as the one taken by said Company.

SEC. 17. *Be it further enacted*, That when any lands or right of way may be required by the said Company for the purpose of constructing their Road, building warehouses, water stations, workshops or depositories, and for want of agreement as to the value thereof, or from any cause, the same can not be purchased from the owner or owners, the same may be taken at a valuation to be made by a jury of good and lawful men, to be summoned by the Sheriff of the County in which the land required by the Company may lie, and in making the said valuation the jury shall take into consideration the loss or damage which may occur to the owner or owners in consequence of the land or the right of way being surrendered and the benefit and advantage he, she or they may receive from the erection of the said road, &c.; and shall state particularly the value and amount of each and the excess or loss or damage over and above the advantage and benefit ; shall form the measure of valuation of said land or right of way : *Provided; nevertheless*, That if any person or persons over whose land the said Road may pass, or the Company should be dissatisfied with the valuation thus made, then and in that case either party may have an appeal to the next Court of the County to be held thereafter, and the Sheriff shall return to the said Court the verdict of the jury, with all their proceedings thereon, and the lands or right of way so valued by the jury shall vest in the said Company so long as the same shall be used for the purposes of said Rail Road, so soon as the valuation may be paid, or, if refused, paid over to the Clerk of the County

Court: *Provided*, That the right of condemnation shall not authorize the said Company to invade the dwelling house, yard, garden or grave yard of any individual without his consent.

Sec. 18. *Be it further enacted*, That the right of said Company to condemn land in the manner described in the above section shall extend to the condemnation only of one hundred feet on each side of the main track of the Road, measuring from the center of the same, unless in case of deep cuts and fillings, when said Company shall have power to condemn as much in addition thereto as may be necessary for the purpose of constructing said Road, and the Company in like manner shall have power to condemn any appropriate lands for the constructing and building of depots, shops, &c., not exceeding five acres in one lot or station.

Sec. 19. *Be it further enacted*, That the said Company shall have the exclusive right of conveyance or transportation of persons, goods, merchandize, produce and coal over said Road, at such charges as may be fixed on by a majority of the Directors.

Sec. 20. *Be it further enacted*, That the profits of the Company, or so much thereof as the Board of Directors may deem advisable, shall, when the affairs of the Company will permit, be annually or semi-annually divided among the stockholders in proportion to the stock each may own.

Sec. 21. *Be it further enacted*, That notice of process upon the President, or any of the Directors thereof, shall be deemed and taken to be due and lawful notice of service of process upon the Company.

Sec. 22. *Be it further enacted*, That said Company shall have power to construct branches to said Road, or to connect with any other Rail Road that may be constructed, and any contract that may be entered into with any other Rail Road Company by the President and Directors of said Company, after the consent of a majority of the stockholders first obtained, shall be binding on the said Company.

Sec. 23. *Be it further enacted*, That it may and shall be lawful for the said "Western Rail Road Company" to make and issue bonds to an amount not exceeding four hundred thousand dollars, to be signed by the President of said Company, under the common seal of the same, in sums of one thousand dollars each, bearing interest at the rate of seven per cent. per annum, to be paid semi-annually in the City of New York or Boston, at their option, and redeemable in the year 1875.

Sec. 24. *Be it further enacted,* That to secure the faithful payment of the said bonds, it may and shall be lawful for the President and Directors of the "Western Rail Road Company" to make, execute and deliver to such person, either in the City of New York or Boston, as the said company may select and appoint, a deed of trust or mortgage under the common seal of said Company, wherein shall be conveyed to the person thus appointed Trustee, the road, property, income and franchises of said Company, acquired or to be acquired, conditioned for the payment of the interest and final redemption of said bonds.

Sec. 25. *Be it further enacted,* That all the officers of the Company and servants and persons in the actual employment of the Company, be and they are hereby exempt from performing ordinary militia duty, working on public roads and serving as jurors.

Sec. 26. *Be it further enacted,* That all the work hereby required shall be executed with due diligence, and if [it] be not commenced within four years after the ratification of this act, then this charter shall be void.

Sec. 27. *Be it further enacted,* That this act shall be in force from and after its ratification, and shall be regarded as a public act, and be continued in force until the year nineteen hundred.

Ratified the 24th day of December, A. D. 1852.

An Act to Amend the Charter of the Western Rail Road Company.

Sec. 1. *Be it enacted, &c,* That in lieu of the bonds authorized to be issued by the Western Railroad Company, under 23d and 24th sections of the act of incorporation of the same, the said Company is hereby authorized to issue their bonds for such an amount, and in such manner and form, payable at such time and place, and bearing such interest, as said Company may authorize; and to secure the payment of the same, they are hereby authorized to make and deliver to such person or persons as they may select, a mortgage or mortgages on all the real and personal estate of the same, together with all their franchises and privileges.

Sec. 2. *Be it further enacted,* That the justices of the county court of any county, or the authorities of any incorporated town in this State, shall have full power and authority to subscribe to the stock of said Company to the amount they shall be authorized to do by the inhabitants of said county or town; and they may issue bonds or other evidences of debt to enable them to borrow money to pay such subscription, at a rate of interest not exceeding seven per cent. per annum, and to levy and collect taxes to pay the same: *Provided, however*, that before any subscription is made, the question shall be submitted to the qualified voters of the House of Commons of such county, or to the qualified voters of such town, and no subscription shall be made unless a majority of those voting approve thereof.

Sec. 3. *Be it further enacted*, That in any suit brought by or against said Company, no stockholder therein, not being in his individual capacity a party to such suit, shall be incompetent as a witness on account of his being a stockholder in the same.

Sec. 4. *Be it further enacted*, That so much of the 6th section of the charter as requires the stockholders annually to elect a treasurer, be repealed, and that hereafter the treasurer shall be appointed by and be amenable to the board of directors.

Sec. 5. *Be it further enacted*, That the said Western Railroad Company be authorized to acquire, either by purchase or otherwise, in the coalfields on Deep River, not exceeding one thousand acres of land, and to use and dispose of the same for mining and other purposes.

Sec. 6. *Be it further enacted*, That if the capital stock of said Company, as authorized by the charter, be insufficient to carry out the purposes of the same, it may be increased by said company to a million and a half dollars.—*Passed* 1856-'57.

An Act to Aid in the Construction and Equipment of the Western R. R. from Fayetteville to the Coalfields.

Section 1. *Be it enacted by the General Assembly of the State of North Carolina, and it is hereby enacted by authority of the same,* That the Public Treasurer is hereby authorized and directed to sell the coupon bonds of the State, to an amount not exceeding four hundred thousand dollars, signed by the Governor, countersigned by the Public Treasurer, and sealed with the great seal of the State, bearing six

per cent. interest, the principal payable at the end of thirty
years from the date thereof, and the coupons of interest
payable semi-annually in such a form as the Public Treasurer may direct, to be made payable at such time and place
as may be agreed upon by the Public Treasurer; and that
the Public Treasurer shall pay over the said sum of four
hundred thousand dollars to the President and Directors of
the Western Rail Road Company, at such times and upon
such conditions as are herein provided: *Provided*, Said bonds
shall not be sold by the Public Treasurer for a less sum
than their par value.

SEC. 2. *Be it further enacted*, That before the Public
Treasurer shall sell for said Company any of the bonds
hereby authorized to be sold, the said Western Railroad
Company shall deliver to the Public Treasurer the coupon
bonds of said Company for the same amount and bearing the
same interest and date, the principal and coupons payable
at the same time and place as those of the State hereinbefore directed to be issued and paid over to the Western Railroad Company, and to secure the principal and interest of
said bonds issued by the Western Railroad Company the
State of North Carolina shall by this act have a lien upon
all the estate of said Company, both real and personal,
which they may now have or may hereafter acquire between the Cape Fear River, at Fayetteville, and the terminus of said Road in the Coalfields, including that at both
points, together with all the rights, franchises and powers
thereunto belonging or in any wise appertaining, or that
may hereafter belong or appertain to said Company, which
lien shall be more effectually secured by a mortgage duly
executed by said Company to the State and registered in
the register's office of the counties of Cumberland, Harnett,
Moore and Chatham, and for the better security of the payment of the interest upon said bonds until the completion
of said road, the Company shall deposit with the Public
Treasurer good and sufficient bonds made by individual
stockholders, or persons interested in said road amounting
to fifty thousand dollars, to secure the payment of the interest aforesaid, which said bonds shall be payable to the
Public Treasurer, and shall be deemed due and payable at
any time prior to the completion of said road, if the said
Company shall fail to pay the interest on the bonds given
in exchange for the bonds of the State; which bonds shall,
upon the payment of the interest to the completion of said

road, be surrendered by the Public Treasurer to the said Company.

Sec. 3. *Be it further enacted,* That the bonds of the State hereby authorized to be sold for the Western Railroad Company shall be sold as follows: when it shall be certified by the President of said Western Railroad Company that twelve miles of said road have been completed and put in operation, said Company shall be entitled to receive one hundred thousand dollars; when it shall be likewise certified that the iron for the whole road has been delivered at the port of Wilmington, said Company shall receive an additional one hundred thousand dollars; whenever the President shall certify that twenty-four miles of said road have been completed, said Company shall be entitled to receive an additional one hundred thousand dollars; and whenever the President shall certify that the whole road to the Coalfields has been completed and put in operation, and that an additional sum has been raised by said Company making the amount of four hundred thousand dollars, and that the aforesaid sum of four hundred thousand dollars (exclusive of State bonds) has been expended upon said road, then an additional and final sum of one hundred thousand dollars shall be delivered to said Company.

Sec. 4. *Be it further enacted,* That the income of said Company, after paying the current and necessary expenses, shall first be applied to the payment of the interest on the bonds hereby directed to be delivered to the Public Treasurer, and of the remainder, twenty-five per cent. shall be set aside and permanently invested for the purpose of creating a sinking fund for the final extinguishment of the debt; the balance may be divided among the Stockholders as said Company may direct, it being the intention of this act to pledge the whole net income of the Company, in the first instance, to liquidation of the interest on the bonds, and then to provide for their final extinguishment.

Sec. 5. *Be it further enacted,* That the State shall have the privilege, at any time within eight years from the passage of this act, to subscribe stock in said Company to the amount of four hundred thousand dollars, in shares of one hundred dollars each, and upon certificates of stock being issued to the State by said Company for the same to surrender the bonds of said Company which had previously been delivered to the State under the provisions of this act.

Sec. 6. *Be it further enacted,* That the Board of Internal Improvements shall have the right, under this act, to send an agent of the State annually to examine into the condition of said Railroad Company, and to report the same to the Governor and Council.

SEC. 7. *Be it further enacted,* That in case any Railroad Company shall be incorporated hereafter, running eastwardly from the town of Fayetteville, or if the Wilmington & Weldon Railroad Company, or the Wilmington, Charlotte and Rutherford Railroad Company shall ever build a branch under their charter, then the said Western Railroad Company shall join in the erection of any warehouses and passenger sheds that may be necessary to render such connection as perfect as possible, and regularly to use the same for the reception and delivery of all passengers, goods and other articles whatever; and the said Railroad Company shall not discriminate by charges against the Company or Companies so connecting with its railway.

SEC. 8. *Be it further enacted,* That in case of a Railroad being built so as to connect any point or points to the eastward of Fayetteville with the Coalfields, by means of the Western Railroad, then and in that case the depots, yards, &c., of the Western Railroad shall be used in common with such connecting Roads, on their paying a due proportion of the cost of said depots, yards, &c., and agreeing to contribute a due proportion to the repairs and improvements thereon.

SEC. 9. *Be it further enacted,* That in the payment of any interest which may accrue on the bonds of the State, before the completion of the Road, the President of said Road shall be required to make oath that no part of said amount of interest has been derived from the sale of the bonds of the State.

SEC. 10. *Be it further enacted,* That the twenty-second section of the charter of said Company be amended so as to read as follows: That said Company shall have power to construct branches to said Road, or to connect with any other Railroad that may be constructed: *Provided,* that no such branch shall cross any Railroad now in existence, or in progress of construction, excepting the Wilmington & Weldon Railroad; any contract that may be entered into with any other Railroad Company by the President and Directors of said Company, after the consent of a majority of the Stockholders first obtained, shall be binding on said company; and this act shall be in force from and after its ratification.

Ratified the 7th day of February, 1859.

An Act to enable the Western Railroad Company to extend their Road from the Coalfields to the North Carolina Railroad.

WHEREAS, The loan of four hundred thousand dollars made to the Western Railroad Company, by an act of the last Legislature, enti.led "An act to aid in the construction and equipment of the Western Railroad from Fayetteville to the Coalfields," was insufficient to enable said Company to procure the rolling stock and equipment, build workshops, and construct the necessary wharves at Cape Fear River, for the shipment of coal and other produce, and for the erection of a permanent bridge across Deep River; therefore, to enable said Company to complete said works, and to carry into effect the provisions of this act:

SECTION 1. *Be it enacted by General Assembly of the State of North Carolina, and it is hereby enacted by the authority of the same,* That there shall be two divisions of the Western Railroad, viz: the Eastern Division shall extend from the Cape Fear to the west bank of Deep River, near Egypt, in the county of Chatham, and the Western Division shall extend from the west bank of Deep River to a point on the North Carolina Railroad, to be hereafter determined by the President and Directors of the Western Railroad Company, or the Stockholders of the same in general meeting assembled.

SEC. 2. *Be it further enacted,* That for the purpose of completing the Eastern Division, procuring the rolling stock and equipments, building shops, wharves, and constructing a permanent bridge over Deep River, the Public Treasurer is hereby authorized and directed to sell two hundred thousand dollars of the coupon bonds of the State of North Carolina, made in the same manner and form as those heretofore sold for said Company, and the proceeds thereof to loan to said Railroad Company, the said Company making and delivering to the Public Treasurer at the same time its coupon bonds for the same amount, and payable at the same time and places as those of the State, sold for its benefit; and to secure the principal and interest of said bonds, issued by the Western Railroad Company, the State of North Carolina shall by this act have a lien upon the Eastern Division of said Road, together with all the rights and franchises thereto belonging or in anywise appertaining, and upon the estate of said Company, both real and personal, which they may now have or may hereafter acquire, which lien shall have preference over all other claims whatsoever.

Sec. 3. *Be it further enacted,* That for the purpose of completing, the Western Division of said Road, the Public Treasurer is hereby authorized and directed to issue and sell the coupon bonds of the State of North Carolina, signed by the Governor, and countersigned by the Public Treasurer, and sealed with the great seal of the State, bearing six per cent. interest, the principal payable at the end of thirty years from the date thereof, and the coupons of interest payable semi-annually in such form and at such time and place as the Public Treasurer may direct, for the purpose of raising the money herein directed to be loaned to the Western Railroad Company.

Sec. 4. *Be it further enacted,* That before the Public Treasurer shall make any loan to the said Company of any of the moneys received from the sale of the bonds hereby authorized to be issued and disposed of, the Western Railroad Company shall deliver to the Public Treasurer the coupon bonds of said Company, bearing the same interest and date, the principal and coupons payable at the same time and place as those of the State herein before directed to be issued and disposed of; and to secure the principal and interest of said bonds issued by the Western Railroad Company, the State of North Carolina shall by this act have a lien upon the Western Division of said Road, together with all the rights, franchises and powers thereto belonging, or in any wise appertaining, or which may hereafter belong or appertain, together with all the real and personal estate of said Company which they may now have or hereafter acquire, and which lien shall have preference over all other claims whatsoever; and in case of failure of said Company to pay the semi-annual interest on said bonds for twenty-four months after such interest shall become due, or to pay the principal of said bonds for twelve months after their maturity, the Board of Internal Improvement for and on behalf of the State may enter upon and take possession of all the property hereinbefore specified, and dispose of the same so as to protect the State.

Sec 5. *Be it further enacted,* That the Public Treasurer shall issue and dispose of the bonds hereinbefore directed, from time to time, as may be necessary to make the loans to said Company, as required by the provisions of this act ; and said loans shall be made in the sums and on the conditions following, viz : that whenever the President of said

Company shall certify to the Governor that a section of ten miles of said Road has been graded continuously at either end of the Western Division, that the said Company has purchased the iron rails, chairs and spikes, and will forthwith, in good faith, proceed to lay down and complete said section of ten miles, said Company shall be entitled to receive the sum of one hundred thousand dollars; and upon a like certificate, as each successive ten miles has been graded and prepared to receive the superstructure, said Company shall be entitled to receive the sum of one hundred thousand dollars, until said Division shall be completed : *Provided,* That if the last section shall be less than ten miles, a deduction shall be made in the proportion of one hundred thousand dollars to ten miles of Road, it being the purpose of this act to loan to said Company ten thousand dollars per mile for each mile of the Road constructed between the Eastern Division and the final terminus of said Road on the North Carolina Railroad : *Provided further,* That none of the bonds authorized to be issued for the Western Division of said Road shall be sold by the Public Treasurer, until it shall have been certified to him by the President of said Company that the iron rail purchased for the said Western Division is of the product and manufacture of the State of North Carolina : *Provided further,* That the bonds so issued for said Western Division shall not exceed $500,000.

SEC. 6. *Be it further enacted,* That whereas, the provisions of the seventh, eighth and tenth sections of the act of the last Legislature, entitled "An act to aid in the construction and equipment of the Western Railroad from Fayetteville to the Coalfields," are unusual, and have not been imposed upon any other Company in this State, therefore, the said seventh, eighth and tenth sections of said act be and the same are hereby repealed.

SEC. 7. *Be it further enacted,* That the bonds herein provided to be sold by the Public Treasurer shall not be disposed of by him for less than their par value.

Ratified the 16th day of February, 1861.

Resolution.

Resolved, That his Excellency the Governor be requested, and the Public Treasurer directed to deliver to the Western

Railroad Company, the sum of two hundred thousand dollars of the coupon bonds of the State, authorized to be sold for the benefit of said Company, by Act of the General Assembly, ratified February 16, 1861, taking in exchange therefor bonds of said Company, for the payment of which the State shall have a lien upon the Road and other property of the Company.

Ratified 24th day of August, 1861.

An Ordinance to Enable the Western Railroad Company to Complete their Road.

SECTION 1. *Be it ordained by the Delegates of the people of North Carolina, in Convention assembled, and it is hereby ordained by the authority of the same,* That that part of section fifth of an act of the Legislature of North Carolina, ratified February sixteenth, eighteen hundred and sixty-one, entitled "An act to enable the Western Railroad Company to extend their Road from the Coalfields to the North Carolina Railroad," which requires the President of said Road to certify to the Governor that the Company has purchased the iron rails, chairs and spikes, and will, forthwith, proceed to lay down and complete each section of ten miles, before said company is entitled to receive the sum of one hundred thousand dollars, be, and the same is hereby repealed.

SEC. 2. *Be it further ordained,* That the lien created by the said act shall extend to cover both the Eastern and Western Divisions of said Road, and all the other property of said corporation.

Ratified the 10th day of May, 1862.

An Act to Enable the Western Railroad Company to Complete its Road from the Coalfields in Chatham County, to some point on the North Carolina Railroad.

WHEREAS, The Legislature of North Carolina, at its session of 1858 and '59, loaned to the Western Railroad Company the sum of four hundred thousand dollars, for which

2

sum the Public Treasurer exchanged the bonds of the State for the bonds of said Company, taking as security therefor a mortgage upon said Road and all its rolling stock, and property of every kind and description whatsoever; And, whereas, the Legislature, again, at its session 1860 and '61, loaned to said Company a further and additional sum of two hundred thousand dollars, making the indebtedness of said Company, to the State, six hundred thousand dollars ; And, whereas, the interest of the present stockholders, as well as the State, would be promoted by the extension of said Road, from its present terminus on Deep River, to some point on the North Carolina Railroad : Now, therefore, to enable said Company to raise the amount necessary to accomplish so desirable an object, by a re-mortgage of said Road to some one or more capitalists, and an increase of its means by additional subscription to its capital stock :

SECTION 1. *Be it enacted by the General Assembly of the State of North Carolina, and it is hereby enacted by the authority of the same,* That the Public Treasurer be, and he is hereby authorized and directed to subscribe to the capital stock of the Western Railroad Company the sum of six hundred thousand dollars, being the amount the said Western Railroad Company is indebted to the State of North Carolina, and the Public Treasurer is hereby instructed to pay said Company for the stock so subscribed, the bonds of said Company now held by the State, and that upon receiving a certificate or certificates of stock as aforesaid, that the Public Treasurer cancel and surrender to said Company, the bonds held as aforesaid, together with the mortgage on said Railroad and its property, thereby releasing said Western Railroad from any and all liability to the State in consequence of said mortgage and indebtedness.

SEC. 2. *Be it further enacted,* That so soon as said subscription shall be made by the Public Treasurer, and the certificate or certificates of stock of said Company, duly executed by the proper officers of said Company, shall have been delivered, then the mortgage on said Road, rolling stock, equipment and property of every kind and description whatsoever, now held by the State, shall be released, and so becoming null and void shall forever be void and of no effect.

SEC. 3. *Be it further enacted,* That to enable said Company to raise the money necessary to construct and extend said Road to some point on the North Carolina Railroad, to connect with said Road at such point as may be selected by the

Western Railroad Company, or by the President and Directors of the same, that said President and Directors are hereby authorized and empowered to issue the mortgage bonds of said Company in sums of not less than one hundred dollars each, and not exceeding in amount nine hundred thousand dollars, and to be negotiated at not less than par, and not to mature at an earlier period than thirty years, in sums of not less than one hundred dollars each, payable at such time and place, and at such rate of interest, not to exceed eight per cent., as may be authorized by said Company, and, to secure the payment thereof, may make a mortgage upon the Railroad, and any and all of its property or income; in such manner and form as they may determine.

Sec. 4. *Be it further enacted*, That in all the meetings of the stockholders of said Company, the Governor shall appoint any one or more members of the Board of Internal Improvements to represent the interest of the State in said Company, or any individual stockholder, and in the election of the Board of Directors the representative of the State shall elect and appoint four Directors, leaving the President and five Directors to be elected by the individual stockholders, thus giving the individual stockholders the balance of power in the control and management of the Road. Said President and Directors shall be stockholders at the time of their election in all cases.

Sec. 5. *Be it further enacted*, That any deed of mortgage, executed and delivered under the provisions of this act, when registered in the County of Cumberland, shall be binding and valid to all intents and purposes, as if the same were registered in every county through which the said Road passes, or in which the property owned by the Company, and so mortgaged, or any part of it, is situate.

Sec. 6. *Be it further enacted*, That this act shall be in force from and after its ratification.

Ratified the 20th day of December, A. D. 1866.

An Act to Amend the Charter of the Western Railroad Company.

Section 1. *Be it enacted by the General Assembly of the State of North Carolina, and it is hereby enacted by the authority of the same,* That it shall be lawful for either or all of the Counties of Randolph, Alamance and Chatham to subscribe to the capital stock of the Western Railroad Company any sum or sums that may be determined on by the Court of Pleas and Quarter Sessions of the County for which said subscription may be made, a majority of the Justices of the Peace of such County being present, and approved by a majority of the lawful qualified voters of said County, to be ascertained in the manner hereinafter provided.

Sec. 2. *Be it further enacted,* That when the County Court of either of said Counties shall, at any time, determine to subscribe any amount of stock to said Company, said Court shall so declare on the record, and make an order to submit the question to a vote of the people of their County, and said election shall be held at all the election precincts of said County, and at such time as said Court shall order, and the Court shall appoint Judges, and make all needful rules and orders for holding said election, and the Sheriff of said County shall hold the election under the same rules and regulations that govern elections for members of the General Assembly, and all the qualified voters of said County for members of the General Assembly shall be entitled to vote, and those voting for said subscription shall deposit a ballot endorsed " subscription," and those opposed to it shall vote " no subscription ;" and, on comparing the polls, the Sheriff shall ascertain the number of votes cast for and against said subscription, and shall certify the same to said County Court, and if a majority of said votes shall have been polled in favor of subscription, the Chairman of said Court shall make the subscription on the books of said Company accordingly.

Sec. 3. *Be it further enacted,* That said Court may issue the bonds of said County as they may determine, bearing interest at any rate, not to exceed eight per cent., on which to raise money to pay such subscription, and may levy the necessary tax to meet the interest of said bonds, and to liquidate the principal as it falls due, as they shall judge expedient.

Sec. 4. *Be it further enacted,* That this act shall be in force from and after its ratification.

Ratified the 31st day of January, A. D. 1867.

An Act to enable the "Western Rail Road" Company to extend its Road across the North Carolina Rail Road to the Virginia Line, near Mt. Airy in the County of Surry.

Sec. 1. *Be it enacted by the General Assembly of the State of North Carolina, and it is hereby enacted by the authority of the same,* That the President and Directors of the Western Rail Road Company shall have full power and authority to extend the main track of this "Western Rail Road" across the North Carolina Rail Road, by the most practicable route, to pass by or near Salem, in the County of Forsyth, thence by the most practicable route, by or near Mt. Airy, to the Virginia line.

Sec. 2. *Be it further enacted,* That the capital stock of said corporation may be increased to the sum of three millions of dollars, and that, for securing the same, books of subscription may be opened, at such times and places, and under the direction of such persons, as the President and Directors may appoint, first giving ten days' notice of the time and place; and the said corporation may employ suitable persons to canvass the different sections of the State, to procure such subscriptions, and keep open the books until a sufficient amount is subscribed.

Sec. 3. *Be it further enacted,* That the public Treasurer be and is hereby authorized and required to subscribe, on behalf of the State, to the capital stock of the Western Rail Road, the sum of one million of dollars. Said subscription to be paid with the second mortgage bonds of the Wilmington, Charlotte and Rutherford Rail Road Company, now held by the State, and secured by a mortgage upon all estate, both real and personal, belonging to said Company, subject to the same equities the State now has: *Provided,* That said bonds shall be received by said Company at their par value.

Sec. 4. *Be it further enacted,* That the proceeds of the bonds hereby authorized to be subscribed shall be equally divided, and one-half of said amount expended on that portion west of the North Carolina Railroad, and the remaining half expended on that portion of said Road east of the North Carolina Railroad.

Sec. 5. *Be it further enacted,* That the individual subscriptions made west of the North Carolina Railroad to the capital stock of said corporation shall be expended on the western division, as above, and the money subscribed east of the North Carolina Railroad, expended on the eastern division, the North Carolina Railroad being the dividing line between the Western and Eastern Division: *Provided*, That any individual or individuals may at any time direct on which Division of said Road his subscription may be applied.

SEC. 6. *Be it further enacted*, That the President and Directors of the said Western Railroad Company are hereby authorized and empowered to receive, in payment of subscriptions to the capital stock of said corporation, land, in any quantity that may be offered by subscribers, and that the said corporation may have, hold, possess and enjoy the same, and that the said land may be sold or mortgaged for the purpose of raising money in such way, and on such terms, as may be deemed best for the interest of the stockholders.

SEC. 7. *Be it further enacted*, That this act shall be in force and take effect from and after its ratification.

Ratified the 25th day of February, A. D. 1867.

An Ordinance to change the manner of payment of the State's subscription to the capital stock of the Western Railroad.

SEC. 1. *Be it ordained by the people of North Carolina in Convention assembled, and it is hereby ordained by the authority of the same*, That the Western Railroad Company are hereby authorized to return to the public Treasurer the sum of one half million of dollars of the second mortgage bonds of the Wilmington, Charlotte and Rutherford Railroad Company, which amount has heretofore been paid by the Public Treasurer to said Company, as the payment of the subscription of the State to the capital stock of said Company, under the authority of the third section of the act of the General Assembly, entitled "An act to enable the Western Railroad Company to extend its Road to and across the North Carolina Railroad to the Virginia line near Mt. Airy, in the County of Surry," ratified the 25th day of February, 1867: and in place thereof the Public Treasurer is hereby authorized and directed to make and deliver to said Western Railroad Company one-half million dollars of the coupon bonds of the State of North Carolina, signed by the Governor and countersigned by the Public Treasurer, bearing interest at the rate of six per cent. per annum, the principal and interest payable at such time and in such manner and place as the Governor or Public Treasurer may prescribe.

SEC. 2. *Be it further ordained,* That no part of the five hundred thousand dollars ($500,000) of bonds herein appropriated as a loan to the Western Railroad Company shall be delivered to said Company, until the President and Directors thereof shall have executed and delivered to the Governor of the State, a first mortgage on the entire Road and its property; conditioned to save the State harmless against the loss of both principal and interest of said loan.

SEC. 3. *Be it further ordained,* That so much of the third section of the act of the Generel Assembly, entitled "An act to enable the Western Railroad Company to complete its Road from the Coalfields in Chatham County to some point on the North Carolina Railroad," ratified the 22d day of December, 1866, as prohibits said Company from negotiating its bonds at not less than par, be and the same is hereby repealed ; and this ordinance shall be in force from and after its passage.

Ratified the 14th day of March, A. D. 1868.

An Ordinance to Amend an Ordinance of this Convention, Entitled "An Ordinance to Change the Manner of Payment of the State's Subscription to the Capital Stock of the Western Railroad Company."

SEC. 1. *Be it ordained by the people of North Carolina in Convention assembled,* That section second of an ordinance of this Convention, entitled "An ordinance to change the manner of payment of the State's subscription to the capital stock of the Western Railroad Company," ratified the 14th day of March, 1868, be and is hereby repealed and declared of no effect.

SEC. 2. *Be it further ordained,* That this ordinance shall be in force from and after its ratification.

Ratified this 17th day of March, A. D. 1868.

An Act to Amend the Charter of the Western Railroad Company.

Sec. 1. *The General Assembly of North Carolina do enact,* The affairs of the Western Railroad Company shall in future be managed by a Board of Directors, of whom the State, by the Governor, shall appoint seven, and stockholders other than the State shall appoint two. The Board of Directors shall, out of their number, choose a President, and they shall have the power and authority now held and exercised by the present President and Directors. In all meetings of stockholders of said Company, the State shall be represented by some person to be appointed by the Governor.

Sec. 2. The said Western Rail Road Company shall have power, from any point on their Road, to extend the same to and across the North Carolina Railroad at any point at or between Salisbury and Greensboro', and to the Wilmington, Charlotte & Rutherford Rail Road, at such points thereon as they may select: *Provided,* That the sums of money heretofore appropriated by the State shall only be used in completing said Road from Egypt to the North Carolina Rail Road.

Sec. 3. The amendments in this act contained shall be submitted to the Stockholders of said Western Railroad Company, at a meeting to be called within thirty days after the ratification of this act. If accepted by the Stockholders in person or by proxy of a majority of stocks, the Stockholders other than the State shall forthwith appoint two Directors, and they, together with the Directors of the State, appointed as aforesaid, shall immediately enter upon their duties and hold office until the next annual meeting of Stockholders of the Company, and until their successors be qualified. On said acceptance the terms of office of the President and Directors shall cease.

Sec. 4. All provisions of laws inconsistent with the provisions of this act are hereby repealed.

Sec. 5. This act shall be in force from and after its ratification.

Ratified the 21st day of August, A. D. 1868.

25

An Act to Amend an Act Entitled an Act to Amend the Charter of the Western Railroad Company, Ratified Twenty-first of August, One Thousand Eight Hundred and Sixty-eight.

SECTION 1. *The General Assembly of North Carolina do enact,* That section three of an act entitled an act to amend the Charter of the Western Railroad Company, ratified the twenty-first of August, one thousand eight hundred and sixty-eight, be amended so as to read as follows: The amendments in this act contained shall be submitted to the Stockholders of said Western Railroad Company, at a meeting to be called within twelve months after the fifteenth day of December, one thousand eight hundred and sixty-eight. If accepted by the Stockholders in person, or by proxy, of a majority of stock, the Stockholders, other than the State, shall forthwith appoint two directors, and they, together with the Directors of the State appointed as aforesaid, shall immediately enter upon their duties, and hold office until the next regular annual meeting of Stockholders of the Company, and until their successors are qualified. On said acceptance, the term of office of the president and Directors shall cease.

SEC. 2. The said act entitled an act to amend the charter of the Western Rail Road Company as amended in the preceding section is hereby re-enacted.

SEC. 3. Upon the acceptance by said Western Rail Road Company of the amendment to their charter contained in this act, the Treasurer of the State shall subscribe for (in behalf of the State) stock in the said Western Rail Road Company to the amount of five hundred thousand dollars in addition to the stock already owned by the State in said Company, and the said Treasurer shall, for said stock, deliver to the President of said Company coupon bonds of the State to the amount of five hundred thousand dollars, of the denomination of one thousand dollars, said bonds signed by the Governor, countersigned by the Treasurer, sealed with the great seal of the State, bearing six per cent. interest, payable semi-annually, the principal at the end of thirty years from the date thereof, principal and interest payable in the City of New York, said bonds to be issued under the provisions of chapter ninety of the Revised Code.

SEC. 4. On the surrender to the State of five hundred thousand dollars of the second mortgage bonds of the Wilmington, Charlotte and Rutherford Rail Road Company, heretofore paid to said Western Railroad Company in payment for stock in the same, the Public Treasurer is hereby directed to issue in exchange therefor five hundred thousand dollars of coupon bonds of the State of the description afore·said.

SEC. 5. To pay the interest on the bonds of the State, issued as aforesaid, as the same may accrue, there shall be annually levied and collected a special tax of one-fortieth of one per cent. on the taxable property of the State, which shall be levied, collected and paid into the Treasury as other public taxes.

SEC. 6. The said Western Rail Road Company may, at any time, by delivering to the Treasurer of the State, bonds, or other indebtedness of the State, receive a transfer of an equivalent amount of the stock of the State in said Company, and it shall be the duty of the Treasurer to make such transfer.

SEC. 7. That the fourth section of act of the General Assembly, amending the charter of the Western Rail Road, ratified the twenty-fifth day of February, one thousand eight hundred and sixty-seven, be and the same is hereby repealed.

SEC. 8. That for the purpose of extending said Western Railroad from the point on the North Carolina Railroad, at which said Western Railroad may connect at or between Salisbury and Greensboro, up the rich and fertile valley of the Yadkin, between the North and South Yadkin, to such point in the county of Wilkes as the President and Directors may determine, the Public Treasurer is hereby authorized and required to subscribe to the capital stock of said Western Railroad the sum of five hundred thousand dollars, and to pay said subscription in the coupon bonds of the State, in the same manner and form and on the same terms as heretofore provided for : *Provided*, That said sum of five hundred thousand dollars shall be expended on that portion of the Road west of the point at which the Western Railroad may connect with the North Carolina Railroad ; *And provided further*, That the President and Directors may commence grading west of the North Carolina Road as soon as the location is determined.

SEC. 9. To pay the interest on the said bonds of the State, issued as aforesaid, as the same may accrue, there shall be annually levied and collected a special tax of one-eight of one per cent. on the taxable property of the State, which shall be levied and collected, and paid into the Treasury as other public taxes.

SEC. 10. *Provided*, That on or before the day upon which the first coupon of the bonds authorized to be issued by this act shall become due, the President of the above named Railroad Company shall pay to the Public Treasurer, either in cash or in matured coupons of bonds, upon which the Public Treasurer is made to pay the interest under this act, the sum of thirty thousand dollars; and on or before the day upon which the second coupon of the bonds authorized by this act shall become due, the President of the above named Railroad Company shall pay, in like manner, the sum of thirty thousand dollars; and on or before the day upon which the third coupon as aforesaid shall become due, the President above named shall pay to the Public Treasurer, in like manner, the sum of twenty thousand dollars; and on or before the day upon which the fourth coupon as aforesaid shall become due, the President above named shall pay to the Public Treasurer, in like manner, the sum of ten thousand dollars.

SEC. 11. *Provided further*, That of the bonds authorized to be issued under this act, one hundred and eighty thousand dollars shall be retained by the Public Treasurer as collateral security for the faithful performance of the conditions of the preceding section ; and that upon the payment of the first thirty thousand dollars as aforesaid, the Public Treasurer shall be authorized to deliver to said Railroad Company sixty thousand dollars of the above named one hundred and eighty thousand dollars of bonds: and upon the payment of the succeeding amounts named in said section, the Public Treasurer is authorized to deliver bonds to the amount of double the sum paid, until all said bonds are delivered to said Railroad Company: *Provided, also*, That at the expiration of two years from the date of the first coupon of the bonds authorized in this act, the Public Treasurer shall be authorized to issue to said Railroad Company an additional amount of bonds, equal at their par value to the amount paid in cash by said Company in behalf of the State, according to the provisions of section ten of this act; said bonds to be in all respects similar to those authorized to be issued by this act.

SEC. 12. This act shall go into effect upon its ratification.

Ratified the 2d day of February, A. D. 1869.

An Act to restore to the Western Railroad Company its Original Chartered Privileges, to regulate the appointment of State Directors, and to define the vote of the State in the general meetings of the Stockholders of said Company.

SECTION 1. *The General Assembly of North Carolina do enact,* That hereafter there shall be a President and nine Directors of the Western Railroad Company, as provided in the original charter of said Company, ratified 24th day of December, 1852. Four Directors shall be appointed by the State, as provided by the fourth section of an act entitled "An act to enable the Western Railroad Company to complete its road from the Coalfields in Chatham county, to some point on the North Carolina Railroad," ratified December 20th, 1866, when the State became a Stockholder and co-partner in said Company; and the remaining five Directors and the President shall be elected by the individual Stockholders, as provided in said fourth section of the above recited act, and in no other manner; and that so much of an act entitled "An act to amend an act entitled an act to amend the charter of the Western Railroad Company, ratified 21st of August, 1868," ratified the 2d day of February, A. D. 1869, as changes the number and manner of appointment of said President and Directors, be, and the same is hereby repealed ; and the provisions of the original charter of the 24th of December, A. D. 1852, and the amendments thereof of December 20th, A. D. 1866, in relation to the appointment of President and Directors, are hereby re-enacted.

SEC. 2. That in all future meetings of the Stockholders of the Western Railroad Company, the representative of the State shall only vote a number of shares equal to one-half of the number of individual shares or votes cast upon any question where a vote is called by stock. The State's representative shall not be entitled to vote where the question may be upon the acceptance or rejection of any amendment to the charter of the Company.

SEC. 3. That this act shall be submitted to a meeting of the Stockholders of said Company, to be held in the town of Fayetteville, within twenty days from its ratification, upon call of the President, or a number of Stockholders holding at least two hundred and fifty shares, and upon its being accepted by a majority of the stock present other than the State, the term of the present President and Directors shall cease, and determine in ten days thereafter.

SEC. 4. Should the meeting of the Stockholders, as provided in the above section, accept this act as a part of their charter, they shall immediately notify the Governor of the State of their action, and of the time and place of the next meeting of Stockholders, which said meeting shall be held within ten days thereafter; at which said meeting of Stockholders the President and Directors shall be chosen as provided in the first section of this act, and shall hold office until the next regular annual meeting of Stockholders.

SEC. 5. All provisions of law inconsistent with this act are hereby repealed, and this act shall be in force from and after its ratification.

Ratified the 19th day of December, A. D. 1870.

An Act to Amend the Charter of the Western Railroad Company.

SECTION 1. *The General Assembly of North Carolina do enact,* That so much of the third section of an act of the General Assembly, ratified December twentieth, one thousand eight hundred and sixty six, entitled an act to enable the Western Railroad Company to complete its Road from the Coalfields, in Chatham county, to some point on the North Carolina Railroad, as limits the amount of mortgage bonds to be issued said Company to the sum of nine hundred thousand dollars, be and the same is hereby repealed, and said Company is hereby authorized to issue such an amount of bonds, and upon such terms and conditions as they are now or may hereafter be permitted and authorized by the stockholders of said Company.

SEC. 2. That the power granted by the second section of an act of the General Assembly, ratified August twenty-first, one thousand eight hundred and sixty-eight, entitled "an act to amend the charter of the Western Railroad Company," be so amended that it shall and may be lawful for said Company to extend their road from any point or points on the Wilmington, Charlotte and Rutherford Railroad to the South Carolina line, and to connect with any road or roads now constructed, or that may be hereafter constructed in South Carolina, and any contract made with any other Railroad corporation or individuals for the construction and equipment of the Western Railroad or any part thereof, or of any branch or branches of the same, by the President and Directors of said Company, shall be binding when the same shall be approved by a majority of the stockholders of said Company; and said Company may begin the construction of any part of said road or any of its branches whenever the stockholders may so determine.

Sec. 3. That any Railroad Company or any corporation or joint stock company legally organized, is hereby authorized to take or purchase stock, or loan money or credit to, or purchase bonds or other securities from this Company, or in any other way or manner whatsoever, aid in its construction, equipment, extension or operation.

Sec. 4. This act shall take effect and be in force from and after its ratification.

Ratified the 10th day of January, A. D. 1871.

An Act to authorize the Western Railroad Company to open to navigation the waters of Lower Little river and its tributaries.

Sec. 1. *The General Assembly of North Carolina do enact*, That the President and Directors of the Western Railroad Company are hereby invested with full power and authority to open and keep open to navigation the waters of Lower Little river and its tributaries, from Little River Station on said Railroad, to the source of said stream and its tributaries.

Sec. 2. That the said President and Directors, the consent of the Stockholders having been first obtained, are hereby authorized to appropriate of its funds, not exceeding fifty thousand dollars, for the purpose mentioned in the first section of this act; and they may open books of subscription for preference or common stock, make a specific or general mortgage, and issue bonds thereunder, or make any other evidences of debt to such an amount as may be found sufficient for the purpose of this act, and make provision for the payment of the same. The amount expended may be kept in either special or general account, and the earnings appropriated either specially or generally amongst the special or general Stockholders, as may be prescribed by said President and Directors.

SEC. 3. That said Company is hereby authorized to construct and operate all such steam vessels and other crafts as may be necessary to carry the freight and passengers on said stream and its tributaries, fixing the rates for the same, or they may let the same to others, charging toils or rents thereon, but the income shall at no time exceed (12) twelve per cent. upon the capital invested after deducting the annual cost, repairs and operation.

SEC. 4. That said Company is hereby specially invested with power to construct such dams, locks, canals, sluices and other works as may be necessary and expedient to carry out the purpose of this act, and that the rights, franchise and privileges of said Company shall extend from the bridge of said Railroad over Lower Little river up said stream and all the creeks running thence to their source.

SEC. 5. The President and Directors of said Company shall have power to agree with the owners of any land, timber, rock, sluice or other material, and for the operating of the same, for the purchase thereof, and in case of disagreement or for other causes the same cannot be had, then in that case they may proceed to condemn the same as provided in the charter of said Company to condemn for Railroad purposes, and shall acquire title to the same in like manner.

SEC. 6. That all laws and clauses of laws in conflict with this act are hereby repealed.

SEC. 7. That this act shall be in force from and after its ratification.

Ratified the 1st day of February, A. D. 1872.

An Act to authorize the Western Railroad Company to issue bonds.

WHEREAS, The General Assembly of North Carolina has heretofore, viz: by the third section of an act ratified on the twentieth day of December, one thousand eight hundred and sixty-six, authorized and empowered the President and Directors of the Western Railroad Company to issue certain mortgage bonds to make a mortgage on the road and property of said Company; and whereas, in or about the month of October, one thousand eight hundred and seventy, a certain mortgage was made upon the property and effects of the Company, which the Stockholders and President and Directors have declared fraudulent, invalid and of no binding force; and whereas, doubts may arise as to the power of the Company to make a new mortgage, and in remedy whereof the Stockholders of said Company did in general meeting on the fourth day of April, one thousand eight hundred and seventy-two, pass a resolution in the following words, viz:

"*Resolved*, That the President and Directors of this Company be and they are hereby authorized and empowered for the purpose of carrying out the intentions of the charter, to issue the bonds of this Company for such an amount as they may find necessary, and to secure the payment thereof, to make a mortgage on all or any part of the property of of this Company now owned or to be hereafter acquired by the Company, together with all its franchises and privileges, said bonds to be of such amount and in such manner and form and payable at such time and place and with such rate of interest as said President and Directors may determine;" now therefore,

SECTION 1. *The General Assembly of North Carolina do enact,* That the President and Directors of the Western Railroad Company be and they are hereby fully authorized and empowered to make the mortgage and issue the bonds as provided in said resolution of the Stockholders of April fourth, one thousand eight hundred and seventy-two, and by virtue of the charter of the Company, and all acts done and to be done in accordance therewith are hereby declared valid and of full force and effect: [*Provided*, That no bonds shall be issued under this act until the litigation now pending concerning said road and a former mortgage shall be settled.] *That part in brackets repealed.*

SEC. 2. That all funds obtained under the provisions of this act shall be applied in extending the road west of its present terminus in the direction of Greensboro.

SEC. 3. This act shall be in force from and after its ratification.

Ratified the 3d day of March, 1873.

An Act to Amend the Charter of the Western Railroad Company.

SECTION 1. *The General Assembly of North Carolina do enact,* That the President and Directors of the Western Railroad Company, and such Commissioners as they may appoint, are authorized and empowered to re-open books for subscription to the capital stock of said Company, at such points as they may deem proper, and subscriptions to the capital stock of said Company may be taken in money, goods, lands, or labor, and all subscriptions taken under this act shall be expended first in the completion of said road from its present terminus to Greensboro.

SEC. 2. Section one, of chapter one hundred and eigthty-seven, of the public laws of North Carolina, for the years one thousand eight hundred and seventy-two and one thousand eight hundred and seventy-three, ratified the third day of March, one thousand eight hundred and seventy-three, is hereby amended by striking out all after and including the word " provided."

SEC. 3. This act shall be in force from and after its ratification.

Ratified the 10th day of March, A. D., 1875.

An Act to Provide for the Working of Convicts on the Western Railroad.

WHEREAS, The State of North Carolina is the owner of a large portion of the capital stock of the Western Railroad Company, and its early completion from its present terminus at Egypt to the North Carolina Railroad, is of prime importance in order to develop the mineral resources of the State, and to make available the State's investment in said Road ; therefore,

SECTION 1. *The General Assembly of North Carolina do enact,* That the Warden or such other person as may be in charge of the convicts of the Penitentiary, shall, upon the order of the Governor, assign to work upon the Western Railroad at least fifty (50) convicts, said number to be increased from time to time, as the wants of the road, and the number of convicts not otherwise by law assigned, will allow, until the number shall reach one hundred (100). Said convicts shall be cared for and secured by the State according to law, and shall be required to do reasonable work upon said Road in such manner as the President and Directors thereof, by their Chief Engineer, or others acting under them, may require. That for all work and labor thus done, the State of North Carolina shall have credit on the books of said Company at a just and reasonable compensation, and the amount thereof reported monthly to the Treasurer of the State. The amount of such work and labor shall be determined by Engineer's estimate, but shall not be for less than fifty (50) dollars per annum for each convict.

SEC. 2. For the amount of work done under the foregoing section the State of North Carolina shall be paid in the first mortgage bonds of said Company, authorized by the charter thereof to be issued, and until the making of such mortgage and issue of said bonds, the State shall, by this act, have a first lien upon all the property and effects of said Company, to be discharged by the delivery to the Treasurer of the State, the bonds aforesaid to the amount of said work.

SEC. 3. Any Judge of the Superior Court, or presiding officer of any Court, holding their Courts in the counties of Cumberland, Harnett, Moore, Chatham and Randolph may, after the convictions and sentences to the Penitentiary of any convict, order in his or their discretion, that such convict shall be directly sent to work on said Railroad, and report shall be made by the Superintendent of all such convicts to the Warden of the Penitentiary, and receipt shall be given for them to said Warden, and the State of North Carolina shall be entitled to compensation for the work done by such convicts, as is provided in sections one and two of this act: *Provided,* That neither this section or section one of this act, shall have the effect of reducing the working force of convicts on the Western North Carolina Railroad below five hundred (500.)

SEC. 4. The Board of Directors of the Penitentiary shall appoint and fix the salary of a Superintendent, who shall care for and guard the convicts sent to work on said Road, according to such rules and regulations as may be prescribed by law, or by the Penitentiary authorities, [but] the work done by such convicts shall be under the control of the President and Directors of said Company, or some person appointed by them.

SEC. 5. The Board of County Commissioners of the several counties of the State are authorized to work on said Railroad, or to hire to said Company, upon such terms as may be agreed upon, the convicts in the jails of their several counties, and to make any and all contracts with said Company that shall be necessary to carry out the provisions of this section.

Sec. 6. This act shall be in force from and after its ratification.

Ratified the 27th day of February, A. D, 1877.

An Act to change the name and authorize the Consolidation of the Western Railroad Company with the Mount Airy Railroad Company, and to complete the said Roads.

WHEREAS, The State of North Carolina owns a large part of the stock of the Western Railroad Company, which has been preserved by the action of the President and Directors of the Company at heavy expense and pecuniary responsibility to them, and without expense incurred by the State: and whereas, to make the investment a profitable one, it is necessary to complete the road : Therefore,

The General Assembly of North Carolina do enact:

Sec. 1. That on and after the 1st day of March, 1879, the name of the Western Railroad Company shall be changed to the " Cape Fear and Yadkin Valley Railway Company," and said Company under such name shall succeed to all the rights, powers, privileges, immunities and franchises that are now possessed by the Western Railroad Company.

Sec. 2. One hundred and fifty additional convicts are hereby assigned to said Company upon the same terms and conditions as those assigned by act of February 27, 1877, and the Board of Directors of the Penitentiary is hereby authorized, at its discretion, to increase the number of convicts assigned, as the wants of the Company demand and the number of convicts admit. Such number of said convicts as the President and Directors may determine, may be assigned to the work of construction at any point or points between Greensboro and the present terminus of the road.

Sec. 3. Authority is hereby given for the consolidation of this Company with the Mount Airy Railroad Company upon such terms and conditions as may be agreed upon by said Companies; and thereupon the Cape Fear and Yadkin

Valley Railway Company shall succeed to and possess all the rights, powers, privileges and franchises which have been conferred upon said corporation by its charter and the several amendments thereto. And the said Cape Fear and Yadkin Valley Railroad Company may, with or without such consolidation with the Mount Airy Railroad Company, if it deem proper, extend its road by an independent line through the Counties of Forsyth, Stokes, Yadkin, Surry and Wilkes to Patterson in Caldwell County, thence through Caldwell, Watauga, Ashe, Alleghany or Mitchell, or either of them, and connect with any railroad constructed or to be constructed in Western North Carolina: *Provided*, That Patterson in the County of Caldwell shall be a point upon any line of road that may be determined upon up the Yadkin River.

SEC. 4. Upon consolidation of said Company with the Mount Airy Railroad Company, authorized by the third section of this act, or upon the adoption of an independent line west of Greensboro, the President and Directors shall place one hundred of the convicts provided for in this act to the construction of said road west of Greensboro as soon as the sum of ten thousand dollars shall be secured and ten per cent. thereon paid to the treasurer of said Railroad Company, and thereupon section 3 of the act of February 27th, 1877, shall be so extended as to include the counties of Guilford, Forsyth, Stokes, Yadkin, Surry, Wilkes, Caldwell, Watauga, Ashe, Alleghany and Mitchell.

SEC. 5. To enable said Company to construct the roads authorized to be consolidated, or such independent line as may be determined upon, the authorities of any incorporated city, town, county or township in this State, or any other corporation in or out of the State, shall have full power and authority to subscribe to the stock of said Company, or to purchase or guarantee its securities and contracts to such an amount as they may be authorized by the people of the cities, towns or counties, or by the constituted authorities of any other corporation, and may borrow money and issue evidences of debt or guarantee upon such terms and condition as they may be authorized; and the authorities of such cities, towns and counties may levy and collect taxes to pay the indebtedness incurred.

SEC. 6. To ascertain the will of the people of any city, town or county, the County Commissioners of any county, or the municipal authorities of any city or town, may cause an election to be held, and submit the question to the qual ified voters of such city, town, county or township, notice of thirty days having been given thereof in the usual manner; and at such election those in favor of the proposition of subscription, purchase or guarantee shall deposit their ballots "for subscription," "for purchase" or "for guarantee," and those opposing, "no subscription," "no purchase" or "no guarantee;" and the County Commissioners or municipal authorities shall examine the returns made by the inspectors and declare the result. If a majority of the registered voters in such city, town, county or township shall vote "for subscription," "for purchase" or "guarantee," then said city, town or county shall be authorized to make such subscription, purchase or guarantee. The will of any other corporation may be ascertained in such manner as said corporation may provide.

SEC. 7. If at any time during the construction of the roads herein authorized the stockholders deem it advisable to reduce the value and number of shares of the present stock of the company in order to secure new and additional capital, the representative of the State, in stockholders' meeting, may consent to such *pro rata* reduction (not exceeding 60 per cent.) of the State and individual stock as the stockholders may determine.

SEC. 8. For the purpose of discharging all liens and incumbrances now existing against said company, whereby the new mortgage bonds, herein provided for, might be impaired upon the market, and for preserving the State's interest in said road, and for paying off all the expense incident to the litigation in which said company has been compelled to engage to preserve its existence, the Public Treasurer is hereby directed to purchase from the said company $50,000 of the first mortgage bonds of said company and to pay over to said company fifty thousand dollars out of any money which may be in his hands not otherwise appropriated: *Provided*, that the amount of first mortgage bonds to be issued by said company on its road shall not exceed four thousand dollars per mile of road constructed and to be constructed, and shall bear interest at the rate not exceeding seven per cent. per annum, payable semi-annually: *Provided further*, that such bonds shall not be sold except as the grading of said road is completed: *Provided*, that after the expiration of the year for which the present Board of Directors shall have been appointed, the State shall be entitled to five Directors and the private stockholders shall be entitled to four Directors.

Sec. 9. That if the North Western North Carolina Railroad Company should fail to accept the amendment to its charter passed by this General Assembly at its present session, and should fail to survey and locate the Road from Winston or Salem, by way of Wilkesboro, to Patterson in Caldwell county within ninety days from and after the ratification of this act, then and in that case the convicts ordered to be assigned to the North Western North Carolina Railroad Company shall be transferred to the Cape Fear and Yadkin Valley Railway Company, to be worked upon the same terms and conditions as the convicts furnished by this act: *Provided*, that the Cape Fear and Yadkin Valley Railway Company shall, within the next six months after the expiration of ninety days above named, survey and locate said road west of Greensboro or Salem or Winston, by way of Wilkesboro, to Patterson, North Carolina; *And provided further*, that said convicts shall be worked west of Greensboro or Salem or Winston, as the Board of Directors may decide : *Provided further*, that upon the consolidation of the roads provided for in this act with the Ore Knob and Mount Airy Railroad, the convicts assigned by law for the construction of the said Ore Knob and Mount Airy Railroad shall be turned over to the said Cape Fear and Yadkin Valley Railway Company, to be worked west of Greensboro upon the same conditions that convicts provided for by this act are worked on other portions of said road.

Sec. 10. This act shall be in force from and after its ratification.

Ratified the 25th day of February, A. D. 1879.

An Act to amend the Charter of the Cape Fear and Yadkin Valley Rail Road Company.

The General Assembly of North Carolina do enact:

SECTION 1. That of the Board of Directors of the Cape Fear and Yadkin Valley Railway Company four shall be selected from that section of country through which the said road passes west of Greensboro, two of whom shall be chosen along the line of road running up the Yadkin Valey to Patterson west of the point of divergence hereinafter provided for: and the other two on the Ore Knob and Mount Airy line from Ore Knob and Mount Airy to Greensboro.

SEC. 2. That when the grading of said road reaches the point of divergence of Mount Airy and Ore Knob branch of said road and the Yadkin Valley branch the entire force of convicts employed on said road shall be equally divided between the two branches, and continued on each branch until completed to their western termini, and the point of divergence heretofore mentioned, shall be at the most practicable and convenient point on the main line with a view of reaching the Yadkin river at or in the immediate neighborhood of Bean Shoals.

SEC. 3. All laws and clauses of laws in conflict with this act are hereby repealed.

SEC. 4. This act shall be in force from and after its ratification.

Ratified the 26th day of March, A. D. 1880.

[The following acts relating to the Mount Airy Railroad Company, became parts of the Charter of the Cape Fear & Yadkin Valley Railroad Company, under the provisions of the contract, consolidating said companies, viz:]

An Act to Incorporate the Mount Airy and Central Railroad Company.

SECTION 1. *The General Assembly of North Carolina do enact,* That it shall be lawful for Jesse Moore, John Rawley, Thos. W. Prather, Robert S. Gilmer, John Brower, Dr. Jos. Hollinsworth, James Davis, Job Worth, Nick Dalton, or any three of them, to open books of subscription at Mt. Airy and such other place as they may select, for the purpose of receiving subscriptions to an amount not exceeding three hundred thousand dollars in shares of fifty dollars each, for the purpose of effecting a communication by means of a Narrow Gauge Railroad from some point in or near Mount Airy, Surry County, North Carolina, to some point on the North Carolina Central Railroad, either by the way of Salem to Greensboro, on the route of the Northwestern North Carolina Railroad, or by any other route which may be deemed by the stockholders most advisable, and for providing everything necessary and convenient for transportation on the same.

SEC. 2. When the sum of seventeen thousand dollars shall be subscribed, the subscribers, their executors, administrators or assigns shall be and they are hereby incorporated into a Company by the name and style of the Mount Airy Railroad Company, and by that name shall be capable of purchasing, holding, selling, leasing and conveying estates, real, personal and mixed, so far as shall be necessary for the purpose specified in this charter and no further, and shall have perpetual succession, and by said corporate name may sue and be sued, and may have and use a common seal and shall have all the powers, rights and privileges which other corporate bodies lawfully have for the purpose herein mentioned and may make all such by-laws, rules and regulations, not inconsistent with the Constitution and laws of this State, or those of the United States, as shall be necessary for the well ordering and conducting of the affairs of said Company.

SEC. 3. When the said sum of seventeen thousand dollars shall have been subscribed, public notice of the fact shall be given by three or more of the said commissioners at Mt. Airy, who shall have power at the same time to call a general meeting of the subscribers at Mount Airy. To constitute such a meeting a number of persons entitled to a majority of the votes shall be present, either in person or by proxy, and if a sufficient number do not attend on that day then those who do attend shall have power to adjourn from time to time until a meeting shall be formed.

SEC. 4. The subscribers at their general meeting before directed, and the stockholders at every annual meeting thereafter, shall elect a President and five Directors. who shall continue in office, unless sooner removed, until the next annual meeting and until their successors are appointed. But the President or any of the Directors may at any time be removed, and the vacancy thereby occasioned, be filled by a majority of votes given at any general meeting. The President with any two or more of the Directors, or in the event of the absence, sickness or inability of the President, any three or more of the Directors who shall appoint one of their own body President, *pro tempore*, shall constitute a Board for the transacton of business. In the case of vacancy in the office of President or any Director happening from death or resignation, removal or inability, such vacancy may be supplied by the appointment of the Board until the next annual meeting.

SEC. 5. The said corporation shall be invested with all the powers, rights and privileges conferred upon the Raleigh and Gaston Railroad Company by its charter granted in the year one thousand eight hundred and thirty-live, and shall be subject to all the rules, regulations and restrictions therein contained, so far as the same are applicable to a Railroad above designated and are consistent with the provisions of this act : *Provided, nevertheless*, that the Judges of the Courts of Probate of Surry, Stokes and Forsyth counties shall exercise the powers conferred by said charter on the Court of Pleas and Quarter sessions, so far as the condemnation of land is concerned for the use of said Company.

SEC. 6. The County Commissioners of Surry, Stokes, and Forsyth shall have power to subscribe for any number of shares of the capital stock of said Company a sum not exceeding in amount three times the sum subscribed by individuals, and in no event exceeding the sum of one hundred thousand dollars. A majority of said County Commissioners respectively shall at any time within three years after the ratification of this act, determine the number of shares for which they propose that their counties shall subscribe and appoint a day for holding election in relation thereto, and cause the same to be entered upon their minutes, and it shall be the duty of the Sheriff of said counties at the Court House to advertise the object and the day of election for at least twenty days prior thereto, on said day to open and keep open the polls, agreeable to the acts regulating the election of members of the General Assembly, and all qualified voters for the House of Representatives of this State in said counties of Surry, Stokes and Forsyth, who shall have resided there ninety days before the election favoring subscription, may vote " Railroad," and those opposing subscription may vote " No Railroad," and the result of the election shall be made known to the Commissioners of said counties at their first meeting after the election, and shall be made a matter of record. If the result shall be favorable to the subscription, then it shall be the duty of said Boards of Commissionerrs of Surry, Stokes and Forsyth counties to authorize the Chairman of said Boards to make the subscription in the name of their respective counties.

SEC. 7. To enable said Boards to meet the instalments that may be required upon such subscription or otherwise. pay the same, they are hereby invested with authority to issue bonds of their respective counties, redeemable in a period not exceeding twenty years from the dates thereof, bearing interest, payable semi-annually, at a rate not exceeding eight per cent. per annum. and it shall be the duty of said Boards regularly to provide the means for meeting the interest on said bonds as the same shall become due, by levying such taxes annually as upon persons, lands and other property within said counties as shall be sufficient for that purpose, and the said Boards respectively shall have power to appoint one of their number to negotiate any loan or loans that may be necessary, to sell and dispose of the bonds, to receive the tax imposed to meet the interest and apply the same to its payment, and to represent said counties in all meetings of the stockholders of said company and to receive the dividend that may become due upon the county stock, and apply the same either to the interest or to a sinking fund for the extinguishment of the principal as the said Board may direct; and it shall be likewise the duty of said Boards to make provisions by taxation or otherwise for the prompt payment of the principal of said bonds when they shall become due.

SEC. 8. It shall be lawful for a majority of the Stockholders at any general meeting to increase the capital stock of said Company by the addition of as many shares as they may deem necessary, for which they may, at their discretion, cause subscriptions to be received in such manner as may be prescribed by them, or may sell the same for the benefit of said Company, for any sum not under the par value thereof, and the said Directors, or a majority of them, shall, by and with the consent of Stockholders in general meeting assembled, have power to borrow money for the purpose of this act, to issue proper certificates of such loan, and to pledge the property of the Company by mortgage or otherwise for the payment of the same, and the interest that may accrue thereon; provided the interest shall not exceed ten per cent. per annum.

Sec. 9. It shall be lawful for said Company to receive not exceeding fifty thousand acres of land in payment for subscriptions of stock : *Provided*, that it shall not be lawful for said Company, at the expiration of ten years after the completion of this road, to hold more land than shall be necessary for the use of the road.

Sec. 10. That each subscription to the capital stock of the said Company shall be binding from the time of making it. That in payment of the last instalment on each share a credit of eight per cent. per annum shall be allowed on all previous payments from the date of payment.

Ratified the 4th day of April, A. D. 1871.

An Act to amend Chapter 218, Acts of one thousand eight hundred and seventy and seventy-one, enlitled An Act to Incorporate the Mount Airy and Central Railroad Company.

Section 1. *The General Assembly of North Carolina do enact :* That section two of chapter two hundred and eighteen of the public laws enacted at the session of the General Assembly of North Carolina for the year one thousand eight hundred and seventy and one thousand eight hundred and seventy-one be amended so it shall read as follows : When the sum of seventeen thousand dollars shall be subscribed, the subscribers, their associates and assigns shall be and are hereby created a body politic and corporate by the name and style of The Mount Airy Railroad Company, and by that name shall be capable of purchasing, holding, selling, leasing and conveying estates real, personal and mixed, so far as shall be necessary as specified in this Charter, and no farther, and shall have perpetual succession and by said corporate name may have and use a common seal, and shall have all the powers, rights and privileges which other coporate bodies lawfully have, for the purposes herein mentioned, and may make all such by-laws, rules and regulations consistent with the Constitution and laws of the United States and of this State as shall be necessary for the well ordering and conducting of the affairs of said Company. The said Road to be located and run from

Mount Airy in Surry county to Greensboro in Guilford county.

SEC. 2. That section five of said act be amended so that it shall read as follows: The said corporation shall be vested with all the powers, rights and privileges conferred upon the Raleigh & Gaston Railroad Company by its Charter granted in the year 1835: *Provided*, that nothing in this act shall be construed to exempt said Railroad or the property or franchise thereof from taxation, and shall be subject to all the rules, regulations and restrictions, so far as the same are applicable to a Narrow Guage Railroad and consistent with this Act: *Provided*, That the Superior Courts of the counties through which the said Railroad may pass shall exercise the powers conferred by said Charter on the Court of Pleas and Quarter Sessions for the purpose of condemning land and securing the right of way for the use of the Company by this Act incorporated.

SEC. 3. That section six of said Act entitled an act to incorporate the Mount Airy and Central Railroad Company be repealed and stricken out, and the following inserted in lieu thereof: That any city, town, county or other municipal corporation of this State shall have power and authority to subscribe for and take any number of shares of the capital stock of the said Company that a majority of the legal voters of such city, town, county or other municipal corporation may elect to take therein. That upon the request of twenty residents and tax payers of any such city, town, county or other municipal corporation of the State, the municipal authorities of such city, town, county or other municipal corporation shall determine the number of shares in the said Company proposed to be taken by such city, town, county or other municipal corporation and shall appoint a day on which an election shall be held in such city, town, county, or other municipal corporation in the manner prescribed by law for holding their elections, at which said election the legally qualified voters of such city, town, county or other municipal corporation shall be entitled to vote for or against such subscription the legally qualified voters favoring such subscription to vote ballots written or printed "Railroad;" those opposing such subscription to vote "No Railroad." The election herein provided for shall be held at the usual voting places for such cities, towns, counties, or other municipal corporations by persons appointed by the authorities of such cities, towns, counties, or other municipal corporations in the same manner that persons are appointed for holding other elections in such cities, towns, counties or other municipal corporations, and the returns thereof shall be made and the result thereof announced as in other elections prescribed by law. If the result of any such election shall show that the majority of the qualified voters of any city, town, county or other municipal corporation favor the taking the amount of stock so voted for in such election, then the proper authorities of such city, town, county, or other municipal corporation shall subscribe the amount of stock so voted for in the said Company and shall have power to levy and collect taxes, to be levied for that special purpose to pay for the said stock in instalments as the same may become due, or in case it shall not be deemed best to collect taxes to pay by taxation such subscription for stock, then such city, town, county, or other municipal corporation shall have power to issue bonds for the purpose of raising money to pay for such subscription and shall provide for the payment of interest upon said bonds and also for the payment of said bonds when they become due.

SEC. 4. That the said Company shall have authority from time to time as it may deem prudent to construct branches to such points as the said Company may determine, and it shall have the same rights and privileges for the construction of branches as that have been or may be granted for the construction of the main line, and that it shall have the right to consolidate with or make suitable arrangements with any company that now is or may hereafter be incorporated for the improvement of the navigation of the Yadkin River, and it shall have power and authority to extend its main line from Mount Airy through the counties of Surry, Wilkes, Caldwell, Alleghany, Ashe, and Watauga, so as to make connection with other Roads in this State under the same rights that have been or may hereafter be granted for the construction of the main line, and that any city, town, county, or municipal corporation of the State may take stock in the branches of the Railroad or the extension of the Railroad of said Company upon the terms and conditions and in the manner herein provided for taking stock in the main line : *Provided*, that this section (except so far as it relates to the Yadkin River and any arrangements made by said company with any other company or companies for the improvement of its navigation) shall be of no force and effect, until the main line from Mt. Airy to Greensboro shall have been first completed.

SEC. 5. The General Assembly of North Carolina do further enact, That in order to make the labor of criminals convicted of crimes useful and to diminish the cost of confinement of such criminals, upon the application of the President of said Company, there shall be farmed out to said Company one hundred convicts from the penitentiary to work upon the road of said Company on the same terms and conditions as to the management and guarding as convicts are farmed out to other Railroad Companies in which the State has no interest. The said Railroad Company shall bear all expense in guarding, feeding, clothing, doctor's bills, and for the pay of superintendent and overseers, so that the State shall be at no expense whatever in regard thereto, and the said convicts shall not be taken beyond the limits of the State: *Provided,* That there shall be an estimate of the net value of all the work done by the convict labor furnished by the State on the said Railroad of the said Company and that the net value of such labor shall be a first mortgage in favor of the State upon the property and franchises of the said Company. The value of the labor of said convicts shall be ascertained by two commissioners, one to be appointed by the Governor and one to be selected by the said Railroad Company.

Sec. 6. This act shall not be construed to reduce the working force of convicts on the Western North Carolina Railroad below five hundred.

Sec. 7. This Act shall be in force from and after its ratification.

Ratified the 28th day of February, A. D. 1877.

An Act to Amend the Charter of the Mount Airy Railroad and Provide for the Building of a Railroad from Greensboro to Ore Knob.

Section 1. *The General Assembly of North Carolina do enact:* That an act entitled an act to amend chapter two hundred and eighteen of the acts of one thousand eight hundred and seventy and one thousand eight hundred and seventy-one, entitled an act to incorporate the Mount Airy and Central Railroad Company, ratified the 28th day of February, A. D. 1877, be amended as follows:

In section first, line eight, after the words "Mount Airy" and before the word "Railroad," insert the words "and Ore Knob." In line eighteen, after the words "from," insert the words, "Ore Knob, by way of." In line eighteen after the words "Mount Airy in Surry County," insert the words "to touch the Yadkin River at or above Bean Shoals."

Section 2. Strike out section third of said act and insert
in lieu thereof the following: That section six of said act,
entitled an act to incorporate the Mount Airy and Central
Railroad Co., be repealed, and the following be inserted in
lieu thereof: That any township or city, town, county, or
other municipal corporation of this State, shall have power
and authority to subscribe for and take any number of
shares of capital stock of said company that a majority of
the voters of such township or city, town county or other
municipal corporation may elect to take therein. That upon the request of twenty resident tax-payers of any such
township or city, town, county, or other municipal corporation of this State, the municipal authorities of such city,
town, county or other municipal corporation (and in case
of township the Justices of the Peace of such township) shall
determine the number of shares in the said company proposed to be taken by such township or city, town, county,
or other municipal corporation, and shall appoint a day on
which an election shall be held in such township or city,
town, county or other municipal corporation in the manner
prescribed by law for holding elections, at which said elections the legally qualified voters of such township or city,
town, county or other municipal corporation shall be entitled
to vote for or against such subscriptions: the legally qualified voters favoring such subscription to vote ballots written or printed "Railroad," those opposing such subscription
to vote "No Railroad." The election *herein provided for*
shall be held at the usual voting places for such townships
or cities, towns, counties or other municipal corporations,
by persons appointed by the authorities of such cities, towns,
counties or municipal corporations (and in case of townships
by Justices of the Peace of such townships), in the same
manner that persons are appointed for holding other elections; and the returns thereof shall be made, and the results
thereof announced, as in other elections prescribed by law:
Provided, that in case of townships the Justices of the Peace
of such township, for carrying out the purposes of this act,
shall be vested with all the powers vested in the Boards of
Commissioners and the Justices of the Peace of counties, as
to the manner of appointing the persons to hold elections
and so forth, by law for the purpose of holding other elections, and townships shall have corporate powers for the
purpose of this act. If the result of any such election shall
show that a majority of the qualified voters of any such
township or city, town, **or county,** or other municipal corpo·

ration, favor the taking of the amount of stock so voted for in such election, then the authorities, who by this act are empowered to de'ermine what amount of stock shall be taken, shall subscribe the amount of stock so voted for in said company, and shall have power to levy and collect taxes for that special purpose to pay for the said stock in installments as the same may become due, or in case it shall not be deemed best to collect taxes to pay by taxation such subscription for stock, then such township, or city, town, county or other municipal corporation shall have power to issue bonds for the purpose of raising money to pay for such subscription, and shall provide for the payment of interest upon said bonds, and also for the payment of said bonds when they become due: *Provided*, that nothing in this charter shall be construed to exempt said road from taxation : *Provided further*, that when any city, town, county or township, or other corporation shall subscribe money, or pledge any property of said road, the directors or other managers of said road shall not be permitted to lease, sell or otherwise dispose of said road without the consent of such city, town, county or other corporation.

SEC. 3. That section fourth of said act be amended by inserting after the word "Watauga," in line ten, the words "Mitchell, Yancey and Buncombe," and by striking out all after and including the word "provided" in the sixteenth line.

SEC. 4. That section five of said act be amended by inserting in line five after the word "hundred" the words "and fifty," and by striking out in line twelve the words "provided that" and inserting "to this end."

SEC. 5. That the proviso in section four of said chapter be stricken out.

SEC. 6. That this act shall be in force from and after its ratification.

Read three times in the General Assembly, and ratified the 11th day of February, A. D. 1879.

BY-LAWS.

ARTICLE I.

The annual meeting of this Company shall be held on the first Thursday in April, in each and every year, in the town of Fayetteville.

ARTICLE II.

The Stockholders other than the State, at each annual meeting, shall elect by ballot a President and four Directors, the State of North Carolina appointing five Directors as now provided by law.

ARTICLE III.

The President and any four Directors shall form a quorum for the transaction of business. In the absence of the President any five Directors shall form a quorum.

ARTICLE IV.

The Board of Directors shall have power to adopt all necessary measures for the construction of the Road, and in all things to manage the affairs of the Company.

ARTICLE V.

The President of the Company shall sign all certificates of stock and other official papers of the Company; call special meetings of the Board at discretion or upon application of any two Directors, and upon written application of Stockholders holding two hundred and fifty shares of stock to call a general meeting of the Stockholders of the Company; sign all orders on the Treasurer and generally exercise superintendence over the affairs of the Company; he shall only be entitled to vote when there is a tie in the Board of Directors, and his salary shall be fixed by the Board of Directors

ARTICLE VI.

The Board of Directors shall appoint a Secretary and a Treasurer, whose duties and liabilities shall be defined by said Board, and whose salaries shall be fixed by them. The Secretary shall be the secretary of the Company and of the Board of Directors.

ARTICLE VII.

Stock shall only be transferred by a surrender of the original certificate by the holder thereof, or by his attorney specially authorized to make such transfer at the office of the Company in Fayetteville, or at such agency as shall be established for that purpose by the Board of Directors.

ARTICLE VIII.

At each annual meeting of the Stockholders, a committee of three shall be appointed to examine the accounts of the several officers at the end of the fiscal year, and report thereon at the next annual meeting.

ARTICLE IX.

The fiscal year of the Company shall close on the last day of February in each year, and all books and accounts shall be balanced at that date, and in five days thereafter shall be subject to the inspection and examination of the committee appointed by the preceding article.

ARTICLE X.

The form of the certificate of the capital stock of the Company shall be as follows:

NORTH CAROLINA.

No. .... Shares.

Be it known that .... of .... entitled to ....
Shares in the Capital Stock of the Western Railroad Company, on which the full sum of One Hundred Dollars per Share has been paid, transferable by said .... personally or by attorney.

Witness the signature of the President and Secretary, and seal of the corporation, at office, this ...... day of ......, 18....

...., Prest.

...., Sec'y.

ARTICLE XI.

The President and Directors shall from time to time issue full certificates of stock to the amount of three-fourths of the actual payments made by any Stockholder upon application of such Stockholder.

ARTICLE XII.

All By-Laws heretofore adopted by this Company are hereby repealed.

APPENDIX.

An Act to be entitled An act to restore the credit of the State and to facilitate the construction of our unfinished railroads.

SECTION 1. *The General Assembly of North Carolina do enact*, It shall be the duty of the several Presidents or other Officers of Railroads who have secured bonds or other securities of the State for the construction of any road in which the State is interested, under an act of the General Assembly or ordinance of a Convention passed since May, year of our Lord one thousand eight hundred and sixty-five, whether such President or other Officers be now in or out of office, and every such President or other Officer is hereby required to file before the Governor and Superintendent of Public Works a statement showing the following items: First, what amount of bonds of the State was received by such President or other Officer from the Public Treasurer, or from any predecessor in office of such President or other Officer, with the respective dates of such reception; second, what amount of such bonds have been sold, in what markets, and at what prices, with the respective dates of such sales; third, what amount of such bonds have been or are now hypothecated, to whom so hypothecated, when hypothecated, for what purpose, and what amount of money has been realized by such hypothecation; fourth, what amount of such bonds remain on hand unsold, or have been turned over unsold to any successor of such President or other Officer, and whether any interest, and if any, how much has been received by him on any unsold bonds of the State.

SEC. 2. The statement required of such President or other Officer by the foregoing section shall be made on oath administered by any person authorized by law to administer oaths, and if any false particular be wilfully inserted therein, or if any item specified in section first be wilfully omitted therefrom, the party making the oath shall be liable to all the pains and penalties of perjury.

SEC. 3. It shall be further the duty of every President or other Officer of a Railroad as provided in section first of this act, and every such President or other Officer is hereby required to return to the Public Treasurer, subject to the joint order of the Governor and Superintendent of Public Works as hereinafter prescribed, all bonds of the State which have been issued under any authority of law and which remain in the hands of any such President or other Officer unsold or undisposed of; or in case any such bonds have been sold or exchanged for money [or] other securities, the said President or other Officer shall deposit in the Public Treasury such money, proceeds or securities, or so much thereof as he has not actually expended upon his road.

SEC. 4. The Governor is hereby directed, within five days after the ratification of this act, to cause a notice to be personally served on every such President or other Officer of a Railroad, if such President or other Officer may be found or resides within the State, and if not, to publish such notice in two daily newspapers printed in Raleigh for six successive days, calling upon such President or other Officer to file the statement required by the first section of this act, and to make the surrender or deposit of bonds required by the third section of this act.

SEC. 5. The time within which every such President or other Officer is required to comply with the provisions of the first three sections of this act shall be twenty days from the day on which the service of notice is personally made on such President or other Officer, or in the case of such President or other Officer being absent from the State from the day of the publication of the notice to him as provided in the last section.

SEC. 6. *Provided, nevertheless,* If upon the notification of the Governor, any such President or other Officer shall faithfully render the account or statement according to sections one and two of this act, and shall moreover comply in all respects with section three of this act, in every such case upon the sworn certificate of the acting President and Chief Engineer or Superintendent of any such railroad, to the effect that a certain amount of work has been done and not paid for on any unfinished railroad, the Governor and Superintendent of Public Works are authorized and required to join in an order or warrant upon the Public Treasurer, where any State securities may be on deposit, to re-deliver to the President of such railroad an amount of the bonds which shall not be sold for less than sixty cents in the dollar, or other securities or any proceeds thereof so returned or deposited by him under section three of this act, equivalent in cash value to the amount of work so certified to be done on such road.

SEC. 7. *And provided further*, That upon any such re-delivery contemplated in the last section, the Public Treasurer having bonds of the State on deposit as aforesaid shall stamp or endorse on every such bond so re-delivered to any Railroad Company the fact of re-delivering and the date thereof.

SEC. 8. That no special tax shall be levied to pay interest on the bonds which may at any time be on deposit in the Treasury according to the provisions of this act, and the ratio of special tax directed to be levied in each appropriation act shall be diminished in the same proportion as the amount of such bonds on deposit bears to the whole amount of bonds appropriated in each appropriation act respectively; and it shall be the duty of the Treasurer to inform the County Commissioners of the several Counties, from time to time, what per cent. of special tax must be levied on property so as to carry out the provisions of this section in its true intent and meaning.

SEC. 9. If the President or other Officer of any Railroad Company, in which the State is interested within the purview of the first five sections of this act, shall wilfully refuse or fail to comply with the said provisions thereof, every such President or other Officer shall be deemed guilty of felony, and upon conviction shall suffer imprisonment in the State prison for not less than five years.

SEC. 10. Prosecutions under the preceding section shall be brought in the Superior Court of the county of Wake; but upon affidavit of the Solicitor of the State of the sixth district, that the interest of the State requires a removal of such criminal action to another county for trial, it is the duty of the Judge to order a removal of the same to any county agreed upon by the parties to the action, or where the Judge in his discretion may deem a fair trial can be had.

SEC. 11. If any President or other Officer as aforesaid shall refuse or neglect, for the period of time specified in section five of this act, to fully and satisfactorily comply in all respects with the provisions of this act, as set forth in the three first sections thereof, then and in every such case of refusal or neglect, it shall be the duty of the Attorney General, and he is hereby directed to bring forthwith in the Superior Court of Wake County, a civil action in the name of the State, against any such President or other Officer, alleging therein a fraudulent use and misapplication of the public funds, and demanding such relief by the appointment of a receiver or otherwise, as may save or better secure the interest of the State in that behalf.

SEC. 12. The Attorney General is hereby authorized to join in such civil action any Director managing or controlling any railroad in which the State is interested, in case he deems any such Director implicated in any fraudulent use or misapplication of the public funds.

SEC. 13. In case of any process of arrest and bail, or other provisional remedy issued in due course of law against any defendant in such civil action, the bond of undertaking to be given by such defendant shall not be less than the double of the supposed default of the defendant in complying with the provisions of this act; but if the amount of such supposed default cannot be satisfactorily ascertained when the Attorney General or other counsel for the State applies for such process, then the bond or undertaking required of the defendant shall be not less than the double of the whole amount of state securities received by him either from the Treasurer or any predecessor in office.

SEC. 14. The Attorney General is authorized to unite with him in prosecuting any action under this act other counsel learned in law not exceeding two, and the Treasurer is hereby directed to pay, in the manner provided by law, out of any unappropriated funds in the treasury, to such counsel, not exceeding five hundred dollars, for all services under any action or proceeding in this act.

SEC. 15. The Governor, Superintendent of Public Works, Attorney General and the Solicitor of the State for the sixth judicial district, shall be, each of them, furnished by the Secretary of the State with a copy of this act immediately upon its ratification.

SEC. 16. This act shall be in force from its ratification, but its introduction into the General Assembly shall be deemed, and is hereby declared, a notice to all parties of the purposes of the State in the premises; and any sale, purchase or disposal of her bonds, after the date of the introduction of this act, by any railroad President or other Officer coming within the interest [intent] and meaning of the foregoing provisions, or by any other persons holding such bonds on his hypothecation from such President or other Officer, or otherwise, (except as a *bona fide* purchaser) shall be absolutely null and void, and the State will, in no event, recognize any such sale, purchaser or disposal as of binding force.

SEC. 17. In case any President or other Officer, who may

come within the provision of this act, shall be absent from or reside beyond the limits of this State, and shall upon notification of the Governor refuse or neglect to answer or otherwise appear to any action instituted in the courts of this State under this act, it shall be the duty of the Governor and he is hereby required to make a requisition and demand for any such President or other Officer upon the Governor of any State where such President or other Officer may be at the time or in which he may reside.

Ratified the 5th day of February, A. D. 1870.

———

An act to be entitled "An act to repeal certain acts passed at the session of one thousand eight hundred and sixty-eight and one thousand eight hundred and sixty-nine, making appropriations to Railroad Companies."

SECTION 1. *The General Assembly of North Carolina do enact,* That all acts passed at the last session of this Legislature making appropriations to Railroad Companies be and the same are hereby repealed; that all bonds of the State which have been issued under the said acts now in the hands of any President or other Officer of the corporation be immediately returned to the Treasurer.

SEC. 2. The moneys in the State Treasury which were levied and collected under the provisions of the acts mentioned in section one of this act are hereby appropriated to the use of the State Government, and shall be credited to the counties of the State upon the tax to be assessed for the year one thousand eight hundred and seventy in proportion to the amounts collected from them respectively.

SEC. 3. All laws and clauses of laws coming in conflict with this act are hereby repealed.

SEC. 4. This act shall be in force from and after its ratification.

Ratified the 8th day of March, A. D. 1870.

An act to compel the President and Directors of the several Railroads in the State to account with their successors in office for the property and effects of said Company.

SEC. 1. *The General Assembly of North Carolina do enact,* That the President and Directors of the several railroads in this State, and all persons acting under them, are hereby required, upon demand, to account with the President and Directors elected or appointed to succeed them, and shall transfer to them forthwith all the money, books, papers, choses in action, property and effects of every kind and description belonging to such Company, and that a refusal or failure to account for and transfer all the money, books, papers, choses in action, property and effects, as herein required, shall be deemed a misdemeanor, and upon conviction in any Superior Court of this State shall be punished by imprisonment in the Penitentiary of this State for not less than one nor more than five years, and by fine at the discretion of the Court.

SEC. 2. That the Governor of this State be and he is hereby authorized, at the request of the President, Directors or other Officer of any railroad Company, to make requisition upon the Governor of any other State for the apprehension of any such President failing to comply with the provisions of the first section of this act.

SEC. 3. That all persons conspiring with any such President, Directors or their agents to defeat, delay or hinder the execution of this act, shall be deemed guilty of a misdemeanor, and on conviction in any Superior Court of this State, shall be subject to the penalties provided in the first section of this act.

SEC. 4. The provisions of this act shall apply to all Presidents and Directors and their agents, who have not settled in full with their successors in office prior to the ratification of this act.

SEC. 5. This act shall be in force from and after its ratification.

Ratified the 16th day of February, A. D. 1871.

An act for exchanging the stocks of the State for bonds with which such stocks were obtained, and for other purposes.

SECTION 1. *The General Assembly of North Carolina do enact,* That the Public Treasurer and Attorney General shall advertise for six months in such newspapers as they may select, and invite proposals for an exchange of the stocks held by the State in any railroad or other corporation, for the bonds by which the state acquired such stocks, or any other bonds of the State (not special tax) where the stock is not specially pledged for the redemption of bonds issued to such corporation; such bids shall be opened on a day appointed, and those terms be accepted which may be most advantageous for the State: *Provided,* That in no event shall any of the said stocks be exchanged for less than their par value, or for less than the bonds of same nominal value, issued in aid of Chatham Railroad January first, one thousand eight hundred and sixty-three: *And provided further,* No stock in the North Carolina Railroad shall be exchanged, unless in the same offer it is proposed to take twenty shares of stock in the North Carolina Railroad, ten shares in the Atlantic and North Carolina Railroad, and twenty shares in the Western North Carolina Railroad Company (Eastern Division), and to pay therefor two bonds of one thousand dollars each of the State, issued to the North Carolina Railroad under acts of one thousand eight hundred and forty-nine, chapter (82) eighty-two, or one thousand eight hundred and fifty-four and one thousand eight hundred and fifty-five, chapter thirty-two, one bond of one thousand dollars, issued to the Atlantic and North Carolina Railroad, under acts one thousand eight hundred and fifty-four and one thousand eight hundred and fifty-five, chapter two hundred and thirty-two, or acts of one thousand eight hundred and fifty six, chapter seventy-four and seventy-six, and two bonds of one thousand dollars, issued to the Western North Carolina Railroad (Eastern Division), acts of one thousand eight hundred and sixty-six and one thousand eight hundred and sixty-seven, chapter one hundred and six, or in the aforesaid proportion.

SEC. 2. That any railroad or other corporation, which has heretofore received bonds of the State in exchange for bonds of said corporation or person holding such State bonds, shall be entitled to a surrender of a bond of such corporation, upon the return to the Treasury of the State bond of equal amount, issued under the acts of the General Assembly or Ordinances of the Convention authorizing such exchange, and upon a return of all bonds issued under any particular act or ordinance, the corporation shall be entitled to a cancellation and surrender of any mortgage executed to the State for securing payment of such corporation bonds, or State bonds; coupons on said bonds may be exchanged in like manner and cut off and retained on either side to make equality.

SEC. 3. To facilitate the exchange proposed in this act, the State does hereby relinquish all claim for stock in the Western Railroad above one million one hundred thousand dollars, and surrender to the said Company two hundred and twenty-five thousand dollars coupons now in State Treasury, withheld on a former exchange of Company bonds for stock in said railroad; and also the State does hereby relinquish all claims to stock in said Company above six hundred thousand dollars upon the return to the Treasury of the five hundred thousand dollars of Wilmington, Charlotte and Rutherford Company bonds and coupons heretofore issued to said Western Railroad Company: *Provided*, That any person acquiring a share of State stock in said corporation shall be entitled to all rights and privileges with the private Stockholders in voting and in the election of the Directors, whose number shall be determined by the Stockholders of said Company. The State also relinquishes all claim to stock in the Western North Carolina Railroad, above four millions of dollars.

SEC. 4. That as soon as the proportion of shares of stock for which the State appoints one Director in any corporation is exchanged, the right of the State to appoint such Director shall cease and determine, and one Director, to be selected by lot, shall be deducted from the number appointed on the part of the State, and upon acceptance of this act by any corporation and such guarantees given for its fulfilment as shall be deemed sufficient by the Treasurer and Attorney General, all further right to representation by the State, either by Directors or proxy, shall cease and determine.

SEC. 5. That as soon as may be practicable, the Public Treasurer shall receive the bonds offered in exchange, and in the presence of the Auditor and Attorney General, shall cancel the same. It shall also be his duty to transfer the stocks and execute such conveyances of the other interest hereinbefore mentioned as shall be deemed necessary, such conveyance to be in a form approved by the Attorney General.

Sec. 6. It shall be the duty of the Auditor to make a minute of what shall be done by the Treasurer in the premises, and to make therefrom such entries in the books of his office as may secure a just accountability on the part of the Treasurer because of the transaction hereinbefore mentioned.

Sec. 7. The Public Treasurer shall make special reports upon the subject of this act to the General Assembly at every session.

Sec. 8. That this act shall be in force from and after its ratification.

Ratified the 1st day of February, A. D. 1872.

An act to repeal Chapter ninety-three of Public Laws of one thousand eight hundred and seventy-one and one thousand eight hundred and seventy-two.

SECTION 1. *The General Assembly of North Carolina do enact,* That an act entitled an act for exchanging the stocks of the State for bonds with which such stocks were obtained, and for other purposes, it being chapter ninety-three of public laws of the session of one thousand eight hundred and seventy-one and one thousand eight hundred and seventy-two, be and the same is hereby repealed.

Sec. 2. That this act shall go into effect immediately.

Ratified the 3d day of March, 1873.

INDEX AND EXPLANATIONS.

ACT DECEMBER 24, 1852—PAGES 3 TO 9.

SECTIONS 1 and 2. Authorization of the construction of a railroad from Fayetteville to the Coalfields in Moore and Chatham Counties, capital stock, $500,000.

SECS. 3 and 4. Commissioners to open books and regulations as to subscriptions.

SEC. 5. When deemed a corporation, and enumeration of legal power of corporation.

SEC. 6. Regulations of first organization, (election of Treasurer changed by 4th section of act, 1856–'57.)

SEC. 7. Manner of voting in Stockholder's meeting.

SEC. 8. Board of Directors to fill vacancies and appoint President *pro tempore.*

SECS. 9 and 10. Regulations, as to calling stock payments, and liabilities of Stockholders.

SEC. 11. Certificates of stock may be issued.

SEC. 12. Power to increase stock.

SEC. 13. Power to use any part of the constructed road.

SEC. 14. Authentication of contracts.

SEC. 15. Power to purchase and hold real estate.

SEC. 16. Power to cross public roads.

SECS. 17 and 18. Condemnation of right of way and all necessary lands for use of road.

SEC. 19. Exclusive right of transportation and charges.

SEC. 20. Dividends.

SEC. 21. Service of process.

SEC. 22. Power to construct branches and make contracts with other railroads.

SECS. 23 and 24. Power to issue bonds and execute mortgage (amended by 1st section of act 1856–'57.)

SEC. 25. Exemption of officers and employees from militia duty, &c.

SEC. 26. Work to begin in four years, and due diligence required.

SEC. 27. When in force.

6 4

ACT 1856-'57—Page 9.

Sec. 1. Repeals 23d and 24th sections of act December 24th, 1852, in relation to mortgage and grants new powers.
Sec. 2. Allows counties and towns to subscribe.
Sec. 3. Stockholders may be witnesses.
Sec. 4. Repeals 6th section of act 1852, as to appointment of Treasurer.
Sec. 5. Authority to acquire coal lands.
Sec. 6. Power to increase capital stock.

ACT FEBRUARY 7, 1859—Pages 10 to 13.

Secs. 1, 2 and 3. Authorizes exchange of $400,000 of bonds of State for Company bonds and regulates the exchange. (These bonds, by act of December 20, 1866, were exchanged for the stock of the Company.)
Sec. 4. Application of income.
Sec. 5. State may exchange bonds for stock.
Sec. 6. Board of Internal Improvement may examine.
Secs. 7, 8 and 10. Connections with other roads. (Repealed by 6 section of act 16th February, 1861.)
Sec. 9. Payment of interest on State bonds.

ACT FEBRUARY 16, 1861—Pages 14 to 16.

Sec. 1. Extension of road to some point on North Carolina Railroad.
Secs. 2, 3, 4, 5 and 7. Authorizes exchange of Company bonds for $200,000 of State bonds. (These bonds were exchanged for stock under act December 20, 1861.)
Sec. 6. Repeals 7, 8 and 10 sections of act of 1859.

ORDINANCE OF MAY 10, 1862—Page 17.

Repeals part of section 5, act February 16, 1861.

ACT DECEMBER 20, 1866—Page 17.

Secs. 1 and 2. State exchanges $600,000 of Company bonds for stock and releases Company of all liability under mortgage.
Sec. 3. Authorizes new mortgage for $900,000. (Amended by act of 1871.)
Sec. 4. State proxy and appointment of Directors.
Sec. 5. Registration of mortgage deed.

ACT JANUARY 31, 1867—PAGE 19.

Authorizes Randolph, Alamance and Chatham county to subscribe.

ACT FEBRUARY 25, 1867—PAGE 21.

SEC. 1. Extends road via Salem and Mt. Airy to Virginia line.
SEC. 2. Increases capital stock to three millions.
SECS. 3 and 4. State subscribes one millon payable in Wilmington, Charlotte and Rutherford Railroad bonds.
SEC. 5. How individual subscriptions are to be applied.
SEC. 6. Allows subscriptions to be paid in land.

ORDINANCE MARCH 14, 1868—PAGE 22.

SEC. 1. $500,000 of Wilmington, Charlotte and Rutherford Railroad bonds exchanged for State bonds.
SEC. 2. Repealed by section 1, Ordinance of March 17, 1868.
SEC. 3. Negotiation of Company bonds at par repealed.

ACT AUGUST 21, 1868—PAGE 24.

SEC. 1. State appoints seven Directors, Stockholders two Directors. (Repealed by act December 19, 1870.)
SEC. 2. Power to cross the North Carolina Railroad, and to extend to Wilmington, Charlotte and Rutherford Railroad. (Amended by act January, 1871.)
SEC. 3. Amendments to be submitted to Stockholders.

ACT FEBRUARY 2, 1869—PAGE 25.

All the sections of this act, except 6 and 7, repealed by act December 19, 1870.

ACT DECEMBER 19, 1870—PAGE 28.

SEC. 1. State appoints four Directors, individuals five Directors. (Amended by act February 25, 1879.)
SEC 2 How State shall vote in Stockholders' meetings.
SECS. 3 and 4. Amendments to be submitted to Stockholders' meeting.

ACT JANUARY 10, 1871—Page 29.

Sec. 1. Repeals 3d section of act December 20, 1866, limiting issue of mortgage bonds.
Sec. 2. Authorizes extension of road to the South Carolina line, and allows contracts to be made with any other railroads.
Sec. 3. Railroad and joint stock Companies may take stock.

ACT FEBRUARY 1, 1872—Page 30.

Authorizes the opening of Lower Little River to navigation.

ACT MARCH 3, 1873—Page 31.

Sec. 1. Gives power to execute new mortgage and issue new bonds.
Sec. 2. Proceeds of new bonds to be applied on Greensboro extension. (Amended by act March 10, 1875.)

ACT MARCH 10, 1875—Page 33.

Sec. 1. Authorizes new subscriptions payable in money, goods, lands or labor.
Sec. 2. Repeals *proviso* of section 10, act March 3, 1873.

ACT FEBRUARY 27, 1877—Page 33.

Secs. 1 and 2. Provides for working of convicts, and for payment of same.
Sec. 3. Gives power to courts of certain counties to assign convicts direct to the Company.
Sec. 4. Appointment and salary of Superintendent of Convicts.
Sec. 5. County Commissioners authorized to hire convicts to Company.

ACT FEBRUARY 25, 1879—Page 35.

Sec. 1. Change of name.
Sec. 2. 150 additional convicts assigned.
Sec. 3. Authorizes consolidation with Mount Airy Railroad, and construction of an independent line.
Sec. 4. 100 other convicts, assigned to work west of Greensboro, and 3d section of act February 27, 1877, extended to other counties.

Secs. 5 and 6. Cities, towns, counties and townships authorized to subscribe after elections held and prescribe manner of election.

Sec. 7. Scaling of stock authorized.

Sec. 8. State to purchase $50,000 of mortgage bonds on certain conditions, and to appoint five of nine Directors.

Sec. 9. Provides the assignment of the convicts of the North-Western and Mount Airy and Ore Knob convicts to the Cape Fear and Yadkin Valley Railway in certain contingencies.

ACT MARCH 26, 1880—Page 39.

Sec. 1. Prescribes the residences of the State Directors.

Sec. 2. Provides for the division of the convicts at a certain point.

Reference can be had to acts relating to Mount Airy acts, now part of Cape Fear and Yadkin Valley Charter—Pages 39 to 48.

BY-LAWS—Pages 49 to 51.

Reference is made to Appendix for certain acts, wherein thisCompany was interested when said acts were in force.

www.ingramcontent.com/pod-product-compliance
Lightning Source LLC
Chambersburg PA
CBHW021535270326
41930CB00008B/1260